HEATHENS

CRADLEY HEATH SPEEDWAY

1947-1976

Peter Foster

First published 2002

PUBLISHED IN THE UNITED KINGDOM BY:

Tempus Publishing Ltd
The Mill, Brimscombe Port
Stroud, Gloucestershire GL5 2QG

PUBLISHED IN THE UNITED STATES OF AMERICA BY:

Tempus Publishing Inc.
2A Cumberland Street
Charleston, SC 29401

Tempus books are available in France and Germany
from the following addresses:

Tempus Publishing Group   Tempus Publishing Group
21 Avenue de la République   Hockheimer Strasse 59
37300 Joué-lès-Tours   D-99094 Erfurt
FRANCE   GERMANY

British Library Cataloguing in Publication Data.
A catalogue record for this book is available from the British Library.

ISBN 0 7524 2704 0

Typesetting and origination by Tempus Publishing.
PRINTED AND BOUND IN GREAT BRITAIN.

HEATHENS
CRADLEY HEATH SPEEDWAY

1947-1976

CONTENTS

INTRODUCTION

En route to Dudley Wood Stadium from Cradley Heath High Street, one passes a motor-cycle shop, next door to which is a factory wall displaying graffiti, daubed in white paint, which informs us that 'Ivor is a bastard'. A few yards down the road, more graffiti, on a brick-built bridge, gives us an alternative point of view, proclaiming that 'Ivor is King'.

The uninformed could be excused for asking 'Who the hell is Ivor?' Both statements, a legacy from the 1960s, are testimony to the rivalry that existed between Cradley Heathens and Wolverhampton Wolves speedway teams and are indicative of the passions that arose when these two teams met on the track.

Ivor, either the bastard or the king, depending upon which side of the fence you stood, was Ivor Brown, and it is a measure of the impact that he made on local speedway that his name remains part of Cradley folklore to this day. Over the years, thousands and thousands of faithful supporters have walked past that timeworn graffiti on their way to Dudley Wood – the home of the Heathens. It now remains as one of the few reminders of speedway in Cradley Heath.

Cradley Heath is a 'one-horse town' in the heart of the Black Country, whose main claim to fame in the last century had been its chain-makers, of which there were hundreds. The town had very little to offer in the way of entertainment, and if a first-class sporting event was what you wanted to see – a football match for example – you'd need to make the journey to Wolverhampton, West Bromwich, Birmingham or Aston Villa. Most other sports of a high calibre were just not available in the area.

And yet, at Dudley Wood Stadium over the years, we saw the very best that the sport of speedway had to offer. The very best riders from around the globe, the crème de la crème, the all-time greats, entertained us week in and week out at Dudley Wood. Not only that, but in later years, a lot of the top boys in the sport were actually Cradley riders. During the 1980s, Cradley boasted the individual World Champion on no fewer than five occasions out of a possible ten.

Cradley Heath became famous the world over, not only for its now almost extinct chain industry but for its speedway. Over the years, Cradley has been represented by riders from all over the world, and the riders were revered by the supporters just as much as the performers in any other sport. Support was just as fanatical as football, but without the hooliganism. Speedway supporters are amongst the most kind and genial of sports fans, and Cradley had more than its fair share of them. In the main, they were knowledgeable and passionate in their support and, come rain or shine, week after week, the die-hards were out on the terraces paying homage to their beloved Heathens.

Speedway was enjoying a boom when it was first introduced to Cradley Heath in 1947. Birmingham had had a team the previous year, but with travelling much more difficult in those days, it is true to say that most of the people who turned up at Dudley Wood Stadium on 21 June 1947 had never before witnessed a speedway match. And how they turned out – 12,000 of them in fact – to see a Cradley team made up from youngsters from a local training school. The obsession had begun; the obsession that caused sane men and women to walk miles in all weathers to see four blokes ride around a dirt track on motorbikes.

Cradley enjoyed good support in the early years but, more importantly, they found their first star in Alan Hunt. Hunt progressed from being a raw novice in 1947 to being one of the most accomplished riders in the sport and the fans worshipped him, just as they would do Penhall and Gundersen in later years.

Cradley enjoyed early success, twice finishing as runners-up in the Third Division before being promoted to the Second Division in 1949. Even so, they always lived in the shadow of neighbouring Birmingham, who had been promoted to the First Division and were now hosts to the finest that speedway had to offer. Every now and then, the Cradley supporters tasted racing of a higher calibre, either when Cradley took on a First Division team in a challenge match, or when a special match race featuring one of the top stars was arranged, but in the main the 'Top Dogs' did not ride at Dudley Wood, and would not do so for many years to come.

As Britain began to re-build after the war, so entertainment became more varied and easily available, and speedway, as a whole, suffered. There was an outcry at Cradley at the end of 1950 when Hunt was transferred to Birmingham, but the move was inevitable – the man had outgrown the Heathens. Predictably, attendances fell and continued to do so until the end of 1952, when they pulled the plug and speedway ended at Dudley Wood.

The sport struggled on, hanging on by its fingertips until 1960, when the Provincial League was formed, breathing life into the old dog and bringing about a revival in the sport. The Provincial League was instigated to breed young riders that would one day be the stars of speedway. The top riders in the sport had their own league – the National League.

Cradley elected to be part of the new Provincial League and speedway was re-introduced at Dudley Wood in April 1960. Ex-Heathen Phil Malpass was to be the first team manager, and the team was largely comprised of riders that he had chosen from a winter training school. However, once more it was 'second-class' racing at Dudley Wood and if it was the top boys that you wanted to see, then the nearest venue was at Brandon, where National League side Coventry played host to the likes of Ove Fundin, Barry Briggs and Ronnie Moore.

Support for the Heathens was initially encouraging, although it must be said that before the introduction of Harry Bastable halfway through 1960, Cradley had a distinctly amateurish look about them. The close season saw the Cradley management make a signing that was to be a milestone in the club's history, and not even they could imagine the impact the Ivor Brown would have on the sport. He became master of the Provincial League and one of the most controversial characters that the sport had ever seen. He was idolised at Cradley, just as Hunt had been before him, and his appearance at any track in the country guaranteed punters through the turnstiles. It was with Brown's arrival that the legendary rivalry between Cradley and Wolverhampton began, which continued to thrive over a period of some thirty years.

In 1965 amalgamation was announced, with all teams coming under the umbrella of a single league – the newly-formed British League. For the first time ever, the Cradley supporters would see the very best riders that the sport had to offer on a regular basis. The thought of 'Brownie' lining up at the tapes with the likes of Fundin and Briggs was, to say the least, very appealing, but Ivor was badly injured early on in the season and, although he returned and served the Heathens for a few more seasons, he was never the same rider after his accident.

Amalgamation had been brought in primarily to save the National League clubs, but, as expected, they were reluctant to let any of their star riders go when it came to sorting out team strengths. The result of this was that some of the old Provincial League teams, including Cradley, were very weak. Being without Brown for a considerable amount of time was too much of a disadvantage for the Heathens, and they finished bottom of the National League in their inaugural year.

For the next few years the Black Country team struggled, continually seeking a new rider to replace Brown as they faced the top riders in the world every week. However, the sport was rapidly changing due to an influx of foreign riders into the new league and, during the late 1960s, it was to be one such foreigner who would become the Heathens first true world-class rider – the Swede Bernt Persson. He gave the fans something to be proud of by carrying the name of Cradley Heath into the Speedway World Final for the first time ever.

ACKNOWLEDGEMENTS

There are many people to thank for their help in writing this book.

Unsung heroes Les Pottinger and Mr and Mrs Derek Pugh were the first people contacted, and they gave me permission to reproduce the Cradley programme covers in the book. All of the Cradley Heath programmes were poured over for hours to try and ensure that any details included in *Heathens* were correct, and all of the programme compilers and contributers over the years deserve thanks for their input.

Photographs are an improtant part of all non-fiction journals, and first of all I would like to pay tribute to *The Speedway Star* for allowing me to use some of their archive photographs. Mike Patrick has also contribued to the book. Photographer John Hall was especially helpful, giving me access to his entire collection of photos, and, over the weeks, he spent many hours in his loft sorting through his negatives for anything he thought might be of use to me. Most of the photographs in this first volume were supplied by Cradley supporters, and whilst I am grateful for their generosity, I also regret that I have no way of knowing who they were taken by and cannot officially acknowledge them.

A special mention should go to friends and supporters Nigel Nickin and Alan Hunt for the pre-1960s material that they gave me access to. My appreciation is also given to Phil and Steve Johnson who run the excellent Cradley website at the following address: www.cradleyspeedway.co.uk. They have been associates for many years and, with regards to information, never fail me in my hour of need. Final thanks go to Kevin Barnbrook for his help and encouragement throughout the project.

1

THE BEGINNING
1947

Speedway began in Australia in 1923, but it was another five years before the first official meeting took place in England at the Kings Oak Hotel in Epping Forest. It was welcomed with great enthusiasm by a crowd of more than 30,000 spectators, who enjoyed every minute of the racing on a track laid out on an old sports field at the rear of the hotel. The date was 19 February 1928 and, within a few months, other equally well-attended meetings were held as far afield as Blackpool and Stamford Bridge.

In subsequent years, speedway continued to attract large crowds with the formation of more than twenty teams from towns and cities all over the United Kingdom. Birmingham even had two tracks – one at Perry Barr and another at Hall Green – and other Midland venues included Coventry, Leicester and Nottingham.

Cradley Heath was first considered a possible site for speedway as far back as 1936 when Mr George Bridgewater, of the Victoria Brewery, applied to the local council for a stadium licence. At first he was turned down (three times in fact) before the council eventually granted him a licence to run both speedway and greyhound racing in 1939. Work had already begun clearing the derelict fairground site at the rear of the Victoria brewery when the outbreak of the Second World War bought proceedings to a halt.

During the first year of post-war speedway in 1946, almost all tracks were able to claim record attendances, with over 6.5 million people flocking to the twelve League tracks. Even before the season had ended, the Speedway Control Board announced its plans to form a new Third Division for junior-grade riders. This was the signal for Bridgewater to renew his application for a speedway licence and to form an association with Les Marshall, who was the promoter at Birmingham at the time.

A training school for novice riders was opened at Perry Barr under the direction of former international star rider, Harold 'Tiger' Stevenson. Since time was short, it was a high-pressure course, and Stevenson had to produce enough riders for both the Stoke and Cradley Heath teams. He pushed his protégés hard, despite the dreadful weather conditions, and the youngsters slowly learnt the art of broadsiding on the black cinder track. The stadium at Dudley Wood was progressing too. The shape and size of the track had been modelled on the famous Wembley circuit, but progress was being held back by frequent heavy snow showers. Soon it became obvious that it would not be ready for the opening of the 1947 season in April.

Only a few weeks earlier, the council had refused to grant a speedway licence, following talk of local opposition to the track. However, after a meeting in the local school in Dudley Wood Road, and the presentation of a petition signed by hundreds of residents at a subsequent meeting of the local authority, the original decision was rescinded. However, this was subject to certain Government restrictions on artificial lighting though, and consequently Cradley Heath would only be allowed to run speedway on Saturday afternoons between May and September.

Les Marshall, the promoter at Second Division Birmingham, became the first speedway manager at Dudley Wood, and one of his first duties was to appoint former grass-track rider George Buck as Cradley's first team manager. George had gained many years of experience in a similar position at Perry Barr and he proved to be a very shrewd manager, with a sound knowledge of speedway rules and regulations.

Stevenson was sorting out the novice riders at the training school, and it soon became obvious that the best of the bunch were Alan Hunt, Phil Malpass, Eric Irons and Arthur Abbott. Two of these, Malpass and Irons, were chosen to represent Cradley in the first match of the season on 30 April 1947 at Tamworth. It was a Best Pairs meeting featuring riders from Tamworth, Norwich, Wombwell, Stoke, Southampton and Cradley. The Cradley pair did very well, even though it was their first appearance on the Fazeley circuit. Phil scored 7 points and Eric 5 – enough for them to finish in third place.

On 8 May, the newly-built Sun Street Stadium at Stoke was opened for speedway for the first time with a challenge match between Stoke and Cradley Heath. The Stoke team, with the advantage of regular practice on their own track, were able to win fairly easily, but in the later stages, after mastering the peculiarities of the track, the Cradley youngsters fought back and were by no means disgraced by the 33-48 score. The Cradley scorers were as follows: Eric Irons (7), Phil Malpass (7), Arthur Abbott (7), A. Rawlingson (5), Tom Johnson (4), G. Rawlingson (2), Jack Bishop (1), Alan Hunt (0).

On 26 May, Cradley, once again visited Tamworth for another challenge match, which they lost 31-48. Eric Irons was again the top scorer, but it was obvious that the team needed strengthening before their League campaign began, so Les Marshall brought in four riders who had experience with Birmingham. They were the Beaumont brothers, Les and Ray from Herefordshire; Jimmy Wright, a former grass-track rider; and Geoff Bennett, who had learned to ride a speedway bike on the army tracks in Germany.

Their presence was felt immediately as Cradley began their League programme with a tour of the southern tracks, winning their first ever League match at Plymouth by 2 points. Les Beaumont was named as the Cradley skipper, and he set a fine example by pushing his bike for a lap and a half after he fell chasing Plymouth's star rider Ivan Kessell. Brother Ray and Plymouth's Doug Bell had fallen earlier in the race, and the 2 points gained by Les in 'pushing for home' ultimately proved to be decisive.

Two days later they were 'rained off' at Eastbourne, and went on to complete the southern tour by losing at both Exeter and Wombwell.

Saturday 21 June was a milestone in Cradley Heath speedway history, as the gates of Dudley Wood Stadium were opened for speedway for the very first time. The opening had already been delayed because of difficulties laying the track (due to the inclement weather), but on that sunny afternoon, a crowd of almost 12,000 turned up to see the mayor of Dudley, Councillor Jack Price, open the meeting at 2.30 p.m.

1947 programme cover.

Geoff Bennett – the first rider ever to top the Cradley averages in 1947.

The track was considered by the riders to be excellent, and some super racing followed. A feature of the match was some fine team-riding by the Beaumont brothers, who gained maximum points in the three heats in which they were paired together. After leading Cradley to a 46-36 win over Wombwell, Les Beaumont crowned a grand afternoon's work by winning the scratch race final, setting a track record of 81.6 seconds in the process. Unfortunately, Eric Irons fell in the same race and injured his knee, which kept him out of the team for the next three weeks.

Local derbies always seem to generate a tremendous amount of excitement, and the matches with the Tamworth Hounds in those first couple of years generated just as much fervour as matches against Birmingham and Wolverhampton in later years. The rivalry was built up to fever pitch by the programme writers and race announcers, and the teams, after a hard-fought match, would usually be separated by only a few points. The first of these local derbies took place at Tamworth's Watling Street Stadium, just a few days after Cradley's home debut, and became known as the 'Great Muddle Match'.

At the end of heat twelve, Cradley were leading a tense and exciting match by just 2 points, and Jimmy Wright went out and won heat thirteen from Tamworth's Jack Kidd and Bill Harris, maintaining the 2-point lead. At the end of the race, Cradley manager George Buck protested that Cradley's other rider in the heat, Alan Hunt, who had stalled his engine at the start, had not been pushed to the thirty-yard line in an effort to get him started (as was required by the regulations). The steward then ordered a re-run of the race, to be ridden after the programmed final race, heat fourteen – an unprecedented step.

Heat fourteen ended all-square, which would have meant a Cradley victory, but in the re-run of heat thirteen, Wright was kept behind the two Hounds and Tamworth won the match 43-41. Cradley appealed to the Speedway Control Board who upheld the appeal, and ruled that the re-run heat should not count, reversing the score in Cradley's favour and setting the scene for a great return match at Dudley Wood a few days later.

Meanwhile, Bob Fletcher had been signed from Belle Vue to replace Eric Irons, and he lined up with the rest of the Cradley team the following Saturday for the return clash in front of some 14,000 fans at Dudley Wood. It was a closely contested affair that Cradley won by 4 points, thanks to fine performances by skipper Beaumont, Wright, and Geoff Bennett, who became the new track-record holder when he recorded a time of 81.4 seconds in heat eleven of the match.

The cup competition for the Third Division teams in their inaugural year was known as the 'Midlands *v.* South Cup' (M/S Cup) and was organised on a regional basis by splitting the division into two sections. The Midlands section included Cradley, Wombwell, Stoke, and Tamworth, and Cradley's first opponents were Wombwell away. Cradley established an early lead and held on grimly to win the first leg 51-45, but reserve Arthur Abbott was involved in a spectacular crash and, although he was not seriously hurt, he decided to retire from the sport.

During the first week in July, Cradley played host to one of the strongest teams in the Third Division – Exeter. The visitors were led by Cyril Roger – the eldest of the three famous speedway racing brothers and a man of First Division racing experience. On his first ever outing at Dudley Wood, he lowered the track record to 80.6 seconds, beating

Bennett in the process. But Geoff had his revenge in a later heat, when he became the only Cradley rider to beat Roger in the match. Cradley were, however, firing on all cylinders, their all-round strength proving to much for the League leaders, and they won the match by 16 points.

Cradley then faced the daunting task of attempting to take the points at Southampton, who also boasted one of the strongest outfits in the League. The Saints proved too strong for the Midland team, with future Heathen Jimmy Squibb scoring 9 points. But the fixture also saw the tragic side of speedway as Southampton's twenty-two-year-old Peter Jackson, after only nine appearances, reared up and was hit in the temple by his handlebars, dying in hospital some hours later. Frank Evans, on loan from Bristol, made his debut for Cradley, scoring 2 points.

Eric Irons returned on 12 July to replace Bob Fletcher, as Cradley entertained Stoke, and although he looked a little stale, he still scored 6 points and helped Cradley to a 49-34 win. The star of the match, however, was Geoff Bennett, who beat the week-old track record twice, and became the new holder with a time of 79.6 seconds on his way to an immaculate maximum.

Speedway had aroused so much interest in the area that more than 500 members were enrolled at the first supporters' meeting at Dudley Wood School on Thursday 17 July. Mr Norman Bridgewater was appointed president, Mr T. Cox became chairman, and Mr L. Cox took on the role of secretary.

1947 team line-up. From left to right, back row: Ray Beaumont, Les Beaumont (capt.), Eric Irons, Geoff Bennett, Phil Malpass. Front row: Stan Crouch, Jimmy Wright, Alan Hunt.

The first ever rider parade, 1947. From left to right: Ray Beaumont, Les Beaumont, Alan Hunt, Phil Malpass, Eric Irons, Geoff Bennett, Stan Crouch, Jimmy Wright.

Their first duty was to lay on coaches to take the supporters to away meetings, and the newly-formed supporters' club turned out in force at Stoke the following Thursday. Several coaches of them spurred Cradley on to a 2-point win over the Potters in their next League match, Bennett again scoring maximum points.

Geoff was at it again when bottom-of-the-table Plymouth visited Dudley Wood, the Devils being completely overwhelmed and losing by 24 points. He continued his unbeaten run as Cradley thrashed visiting Exeter. Cyril Roger returned to Dudley Wood to find Cradley a vastly improved team, and could manage only 7 of his team's 22 points.

The beginning of August saw Cradley compete in the next round of the M/S Cup against local rivals Tamworth, both legs taking place on Bank Holiday Monday. The afternoon leg at Fazeley saw the Hounds win the match by 12 points after some tremendous riding by Arthur Payne and Bill Harris. In the evening match at Dudley Wood, in front of a record crowd of more than 20,000 spectators, Cradley built up a lead of 10 points. However, just when it seemed that they were on their way to winning, Les Beaumont fell and gave Tamworth a gift 5-1, which they repeated in heats fourteen and sixteen to give them a 2-point lead.

Southampton held a comfortable lead at the top of the Third Division but, despite Cradley being without Eric Irons (who was injured against Tamworth) and Malpass and

Hunt suffering from bike problems, the Saints were sent packing from Dudley Wood with a flea in their ear and a 10-point defeat. Three nights later, at Bannister Court, Southampton took sweet revenge as Jimmy Squibb, Bob Oakley, Peter Robinson and Bert Croucher were all unbeaten, as Cradley failed to win a single heat and were trounced 59-24.

In the middle of August, Cradley were given permission to run Friday evening meetings for the first time – a pleasing concession with the start of the football season. However, another seemingly insurmountable obstacle at the time was the Government's restrictions on lighting, which meant that the Cradley management was unable to install the necessary artificial lighting equipment for the track. The outcome of this was that apart from one match when it was still light enough to race, they were compelled to revert back to Saturday afternoon racing.

But on this one-off Friday night match, the opponents were Tamworth and, once more, the match attracted a crowd of some 20,000. It was a point to ponder that racing in the week could be very popular, and this way all the fans that also followed football would be able to watch both sports, if they could afford it.

Something else to ponder was the luck of Cradley, which completely ran out as the Hounds stormed to a 48-35 win. Frank Evans and Ray Beaumont both lost chains, Geoff Bennett and Bob Fletcher both seized their engines, and tearaway Alan Hunt was plagued by magneto troubles and failed to score.

Revenge is sweet, and the following Wednesday Cradley got theirs at Tamworth. Coach-loads of supporters turned up at Fazeley to see a very determined Cradley win a thrilling match by 2 points, but a couple of nights later, Cradley had that scoreline reversed when they narrowly failed at Wombwell. The deep and rough track was not to the liking of the Cradley boys, except Alan Hunt who revelled in the conditions and rode to 9 points, his highest score so far. In the return leg the following afternoon at Dudley Wood, Cradley turned the tables on the Colliers defeating them 59-25.

When Cradley visited Sun Street at the end of August, they found Stoke to be a different proposition to the team that they had beaten there in July. The Potters had acquired the services of Vic Pitcher from Tamworth, and Vic proved to be a real match-winner, stringing together five wins and leading Stoke to a 55-39 win. Only Bennett performed for Cradley, scoring 13 points in this M/S Cup match.

There followed a convincing win over eventual League winners Eastbourne. The match marked the return of Eric Irons, but it almost marked the departure of Ray Beaumont whose wheel collapsed in his last ride, causing him to take a nasty tumble. However, he recovered sufficiently to ride alongside brother Les in the second half at Birmingham that same night. Cradley beat Eastbourne 50-34, and the scorers were as follows: Geoff Bennett (11), Les Beaumont (9), Bob Fletcher (9), Eric Irons (6), Ray Beaumont (5), Jimmy Wright (5), Alan Hunt (3), Phil Malpass (2).

As they entered September, Cradley embarked upon another southern tour for League matches against Exeter and Plymouth. Ray Beaumont had pulled out through injury and Frank Evans took his place. Debut man Wilf Wilstead, who had ridden in the second halves at Birmingham, replaced Phil Malpass, who was not available.

As with their last visit to the County Ground, Cradley were slaughtered by Exeter,

Geoff Bennett - two times track record holder in 1947.

Bob Fletcher in the Dudley Wood pits.

Bennett being the only Cradley rider to emerge with any credit, as all of the Falcons' heat-leaders were unbeaten by an opponent. The Cradley boys fared a little better at Plymouth, but were unable to repeat the victory that they had gained over the Devils in June. Plymouth were now a much more formidable outfit, having signed several experienced riders such as Billy Newell, and Charlie Challis, as well as introducing youngsters Vic Gent and Harold Sharpe. Apart from skipper Beaumont, Cradley lacked their usual spirit and the Devils had little difficulty in winning the match 45-33.

Back at Dudley Wood, and with Malpass and Ray Beaumont reinstated, Cradley took on League leaders Southampton. The Saints were without Vic Collins and Peter Robinson, two of their best riders, and Bob Oakley had been injured the night before at Wombwell, but he insisted that he take his place at Dudley Wood. Cradley made the most of their visitors' misfortunes and 11 points apiece from Bennett, Irons, and Fletcher paved the way for a 57-27 win.

When Cradley visited Eastbourne, the Eagles knew that a win would take them to the top of the Third Division, and after a match featuring heavy spills by Ray Beaumont, Eric Irons and Geoff Bennett. Eastbourne sat at the top of the League, having won 58-24.

Cradley knew that they had to win at Stoke to keep their League Championship hopes alive, and Alan Hunt responded to the call, scoring 11 points along with Bennett to lead Cradley to a 10-point win and keep their League aspirations alive.

Hunt maintained his fine form in the return match two days later at Dudley Wood. The Potters were completely overwhelmed as he swept through the match unbeaten and then won the scratch race final from Bennett in a time of exactly eighty seconds.

Alan had served as a deep-sea diver in the Navy during the war, and upon returning to 'Civvy Street' looked for something equally as exciting, hence his enrolment into the Perry Barr winter training school. Operating from the reserve berth at Cradley, he was beginning to show some of the form that would turn him into Cradley's first legend. In those early days what he lacked in style, he more than made up for in fearlessness and determination, and this had made him a firm favourite with the supporters.

Cradley's final 'home' League match of the season was against League Champions Eastbourne, and as Dudley Wood Stadium was no longer available, the match was ridden at Perry Barr. Cradley Heath's St Luke's football team had first call on Dudley Wood from the beginning of October, hence Cradley's last two 'home' fixtures were ridden on other tracks.

Against doctor's orders, Hunt, injured in a recent crash, insisted on riding at Birmingham, and he scorched around the track to win his opening ride in a fast time of 82.2 seconds. It set the standard for the rest of the Cradley team, and a crowd of 22,000 saw Cradley win every heat apart from one to soundly thrash the Champions and gain themselves the runner-up spot in the Third Division.

Cradley's final 'home' match was ridden at Tamworth, and it was a M/S Cup fixture against Stoke. Win or lose, Cradley would not qualify as the Midlands representatives, but if Stoke won, they would qualify for the final. They were emphatically denied by a rampant Cradley team led by a 15-point maximum from Alan Hunt – his first ever.

Cradley's last match of the season was at First Division Belle Vue, as part of a farewell meeting at the Manchester track on 1 November. They took on, and beat, a team of Belle Vue reserves, Geoff Bennett ending the season with a maximum.

It had been a highly successful inaugural year for Cradley. They had finished the League on the same points as Champions Eastbourne, but fewer match points had forced them into second place. They were the youngest team in the League, with an average rider age of just twenty-three, and furthermore, they were the only team in the Third Division with 100 per cent post-war riders.

Geoff Bennett topped Cradley's averages with 8.68 points and skipper Les Beaumont followed closely behind. Although he missed ten matches through injury, Eric Irons still managed to average 7 points, and Jimmy Wright was always in the thick of things, averaging 6.5 points a match.

Although Hunt finished the season with only a 3.68 point average, it belied his obvious potential. He began the season a raw novice – very raw in fact – but kept getting up when he fell. He also persevered with some very suspect equipment until his sheer determination and will to win began to earn him the points he so richly deserved. He had endeared himself to the fans and in Cradley's first season had established himself as their favourite son.

2
THE CUBS
1948

With a successful first season behind them, Cradley looked forward to further glory in 1948 but a few changes had been made. Les Marshall had recalled their star rider, Geoff Bennett, to Birmingham, and Bob Fletcher had been recalled to Belle Vue, only to be loaned out to the newly-formed Coventry Bees. To replace them, Cradley had signed Ted Moore, a former New Cross junior rider, and Bill Clifton, who had previously ridden for Bristol in the Second Division.

Just a few days before the start of the season, Marshall signed up a virtually unknown Australian rider named Graham Warren, and decided to try him out with the Cradley team in their Good Friday 'opener' at Tamworth. In this, his first and only outing for Cradley, Warren clipped 1.2 seconds off the track record in his opening ride, and then went on to score a faultless paid maximum before winning all of his second-half races, including the scratch race final. It was obvious that Grahame was too good to be stuck in the Third Division, and it came as no surprise when, to Cradley's annoyance, Marshall immediately packed him off to Perry Barr, when in no time at all he was beating the top stars in the sport.

Even with Warren's efforts and a splendid performance from Alan Hunt, Tamworth just had the edge on Cradley, winning the challenge match by 5 points. In place of the Aussie ace, Marshall signed Jimmy Coy from Wimbledon, and Jimmy made his debut in a National Trophy match at Plymouth, scoring 2 points. Speedway's National Trophy was the equivalent of Football's FA Cup in terms of prestige, and up until 1948 had been open only to Second and First Division clubs. Cradley's first match in the competition, at a much improved Plymouth, saw their other new boy Ted Moore hit the fence and chip a bone in his ankle, putting him on the sidelines for three weeks. Alan Hunt also injured his foot, but carried on characteristically bravely to score 10 points. However, despite this and 14 points from Jimmy Wright, Cradley lost the first leg by 6 points.

Their League campaign got off to a cracking start with a 20-point win at Wombwell. In order to ride the match, the Cradley boys had to make an overnight journey from Plymouth to the small Yorkshire mining village, but that seemed to have no ill effects and Jimmy Wright broke the track record in his first outing.

The return leg of the National Trophy fixture against Plymouth was Cradley's first home match of the season, and there were huge crowds outside Dudley Wood Stadium prior to the match. Rain had been falling continually, and at one stage the meeting seemed to be in jeopardy, but racing was allowed to commence after a thirty-minute delay.

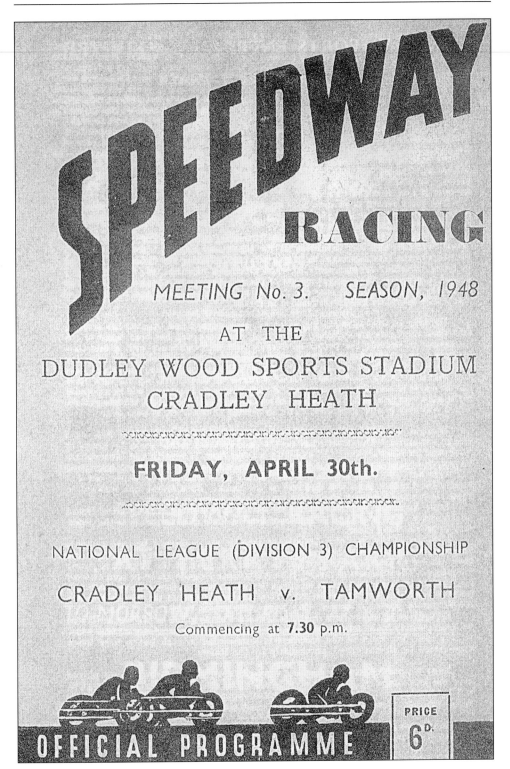

1948 programme cover.

1948 team line-up. From left to right, back row: Eric Irons, Bill Clifton, Gil Craven, Les Beaumont (capt.), Ray Beaumont. Front row: Phil Malpass (on bike), Alan Hunt (kneeling).

Cradley were tracking a new boy. Ernie Appleby had been hastily signed from Birmingham to replace Ray Beaumont, who was having trouble with an old knee injury. Ernie made a fine debut, scoring 10 points as Cradley wiped away the deficit and finished up winners by 24 points. Hunt continued his impressive start to the year by knocking over a second off Geoff Bennett's track record to become the new holder with a time of 78.0 seconds.

Cradley's home League debut was against Hastings, who were last year's League Championship-winning Eastbourne team, and although they had lost riders from 1947, they boasted two of the best heat-leaders in the Third Division in Wally Green and Jock Grierson. Unfortunately, these two were the only riders to offer any opposition to Cradley, whose all-round strength proved too much for their visitors. Green dropped only a single point in the 'race of the night' to the ever-improving Hunt.

On 30 April 1948, the newly installed track lights were switched on for the first time and evening racing began at Dudley Wood in front of some 16,000 spectators. The occasion was a local derby against neighbours Tamworth and, as usual, it was a great match. Cradley were always in control, thanks to the pairing of Hunt and Irons, who dropped just a point all night. Only a broken chain robbed skipper Beaumont of a maximum, and when Irons beat Hounds' captain Steve Langdon in heat nine, it was described as the best race ever seen at Dudley Wood.

The next day, Cradley travelled north to contest the next round of the National Trophy at Hull. Hull were a very hard team to beat at home because not only did they have the largest track in the country, but its 'D' shape made it difficult for visiting teams to master. There was one long straight and one continuous bend, which meant two very sharp tricky turns, thus giving the home side a distinct advantage. Cradley went with the idea of trying to contain Hull and reap the dividends at Dudley Wood, but the home side were without Mick Mitchell, and Alf Webster, two of their best riders, and Cradley made the most of their advantage and scored a famous 66-42 victory.

Jimmy Wright had been brilliant at Hull, recording an 18-point maximum, and in the return leg at Dudley Wood he carried on where he had left off, scoring five wins and leading Cradley to a thunderous 78-29 victory to progress into the next round of the competition.

A disastrous tour of the south coast followed, which saw Cradley humiliated in three matches in as many nights. The first stop was Exeter, where Les Beaumont top-scored with a mere 4 points as Cradley lost 18-65. The next night saw them ride the first leg of the third round in the National Trophy at Southampton. Thirteen scores of 5-1 to the Saints told the story as they romped to an 85-23 victory. Hunt did his Superman act when he hit the grass verge and the impact threw him high into the air. He retained his grip on the handlebars, landed back in the saddle with a mighty thump, and skilfully rode across the centre green, avoiding the scattering officials, much to the delight of the crowd.

Cradley's last stop of the tour was a League match at Hastings the following evening when they fared little better, losing 27-57. They returned to Dudley Wood to lick their wounds and stage their first ever World Championship qualifying round at which over 15,000 fans were treated to some thrilling racing. Alan Hunt was in tremendous form, clipping an incredible 2.4 seconds off the track record in his first outing. He was the favourite to win the meeting, but a disastrous gate in his final race lost him valuable points and he was forced to take third place behind Exeter's Stan Hodson and Cradley's Eric Irons.

Cradley then faced Southampton in the return leg of the National Trophy with an impossible 62-point deficit to overcome. They did get the better of the Saints on the night, winning by just 4 points in what was reckoned to be the most exciting match ever seen at Dudley Wood. Southampton were brilliantly led by Alf Bottoms, who was on loan from First Division Wembley and was at that time unbeaten by any Third Division rider. Hunt once again provided most of the thrills, but this was at great discomfort to himself due to a fall a few days earlier when he had torn the behind out of his leathers and had to have stitches his bottom!

Cradley concluded May by inviting Second Division neighbours Birmingham, along with Graham Warren, to a challenge match and a crowd of over 17,000 turned up for the battle. Eric Irons brought the house down when he beat Warren in his first outing, and Eric went on to be the star of the night, dropping his only point to ex-Cradley rider Geoff Bennett. Although Cradley fought hard, they could not match the superior riding of the Brummies, and were forced to concede the match 34-49. This was the last match in Cradley colours for Jimmy Coy who, unable to find his form, returned to Wimbledon. A few days later, Cradley also released Ted Moore.

Up until now, Cradley were the only team in the Third Division without a nickname, and promoter Les Marshall asked the supporters for their suggestions. The name chosen from the hundreds sent in was 'the Cubs'. This was considered the most appropriate considering that the average age of the team was only twenty-three, well below that of any other team in the country.

The Cubs' 'debut' was at Dudley Wood against Yarmouth and after Coy's departure, local journalist Phil Malpass moved up into the team proper, and his place at reserve was taken by Roy Moreton, another local youngster from nearby Blackheath. Roy made a remarkable start by winning both of his races in his debut League match. Alan Hunt recorded his first ever full maximum, leading Cradley to a 63-21 win.

Three nights later, the Cubs visited Hendon Stadium to take on Hull, and the Angels were unfortunate to lose one of their best riders Al Allison, who fell and broke his arm in heat two. Cradley made the most of their luck and Beaumont, Irons and Wright performed heroics to help the Black Country team to a 48-36 win on a tricky circuit. Eric Irons scored a maximum on the next night at Yarmouth to send Cradley shooting up the League and, with Beaumont and Malpass giving good support, the Cubs came away with a 3-point win and another 2 League points.

Hull came to their return match at Dudley Wood via Plymouth, and having undertaken the 210-mile journey on the day of the match, their tired riders and bikes were no match for the rampant Cubs. It turned out to be a very one-sided affair, which left Cradley knocking at the door of the League leadership.

Cradley went to the top of the Third Division after winning at Coventry in the middle of June. Gil Craven had signed for the Cubs only hours before the meeting and he scored 3 points on his debut, but the star of the show once again was Eric Irons, who rode to another flawless maximum.

Twenty-seven-year-old Craven was quite a character. The Londoner had joined the Merchant Navy at seventeen and his ship was sunk running the blockade in the Spanish Civil War. He gained his first taste of speedway at West Ham, and rode in New Zealand in the winter of 1946 before spending a lucrative season in the USA and Australia, winning enough money to purchase six trunks of clothes (including fifty-five hand-painted ties). He arrived in England in March 1948 and signed up with the Brummies, but with the arrival of Graham Warren, he was transferred to Cradley.

Cradley's closest rivals in the title chase were arch-rivals Tamworth, who had the same number of points but had ridden two more matches. When the two teams met at Fazeley in the Cubs' next match, Beaumont and Irons were both unbeaten at heat nine, but Cradley were 10 points down and had lost Bill Clifton with an injured foot. By the final race, some brilliant team-riding by the Cubs had brought the score back to 39-39, but as Bill was unable to ride in the final heat, his place was taken by reserve Gil Craven. Craven, along with Alan Hunt, filled in third and second place behind Basil Harris to hold the Hounds to a draw.

With Clifton sidelined, Craven moved up into the team proper and Roy Moreton was recalled to the reserve spot, as rampant Cradley made short work of visitors Wombwell and Stoke to keep up the pressure at the top of the table. Alan Hunt understandably 'took it easy' against the Potters, as he was getting married the following day.

June ended disastrously at Exeter. Not only did the Cubs lose by a proverbial mile (16-67), but they lost Jimmy Wright in heat six when Exeter's Bronco Slade was blinded by the sun and ran into Wright, whose chain had snapped. Slade escaped with concussion, but Wright was not so lucky and he sustained a broken pelvis, fractures of the right arm, thigh and collarbone, as well as severe internal bleeding. The match lost Cradley the League leadership to Southampton, who were to be the Cubs' next visitors.

As the Saints pushed hard at Dudley Wood, Les Beaumont led by example, dropping his only point to Alf Bottoms, and Cradley hung on to an early lead to win the match 45-39. But it was Irons who brought the house down when he beat the usually unassailable Bottoms in heat nine.

Hunt had had a quiet time of it since breaking his frame at Hull a month earlier, but by the time Cradley visited Poole at the beginning of July, he had acquired a new Australian frame. He responded by scoring 10 points, leading the Cubs to a fine 45-39 away win. Les Beaumont became the new Poole track record holder.

Cradley failed at Plymouth by only 3 points, but at Dudley Wood the following night, the Cubs got their revenge over the Devils. Gil Craven had settled in nicely and was frequently scoring double figures, but although he topped the Cubs' scorechart at Stoke, his team-mates were strangely subdued and Cradley's championship hopes took a setback as the Potters won by 20 points.

In July, Cradley challenged two Second Division clubs. First of all they met Sheffield at Belle Vue (the Aces were riding away), but the Tigers were without Tommy Allott, and with the Cubs using Bob Quick as a guest, the result of a thrilling meeting was a draw. Craven continued to impress and was beaten only by Bruce Semmens. Norwich were

Les Beaumont in action.

Ray Beaumont.

Cradley's other Second Division opponents (this time at Yarmouth) and, as a mark of respect, the Stars fielded their full team. Only the machine problems of Hunt and Malpass prevented the score from being closer as Norwich took full advantage and won the match 51-33.

Ray Beaumont had featured in the eight-man line-up over the last few matches, but he was not the rider of old and was finding the points hard to come by, as was young Moreton. On the other hand, Gil Craven was enjoying huge success. When title-chasing Exeter visited Dudley Wood, Gil scored his first maximum and led the Cubs to a 50-33 win, and a week later, when Cradley played host to Plymouth, he repeated the performance to lead the team to two more League points.

At the end of July, and in front of the largest crowd of the season at Hastings, Cradley's title aspirations took a knock as they lost 28-56. The Cubs began without Eric Irons, who had been injured at Tamworth a few days earlier, but his replacement, Wilf Wilstead, crashed in the match and was carried from the track unconscious, but he later bravely continued and managed to score a couple of points. However, to make matters worse, Cradley lost Gil Craven when he crashed in his first race, so with two top riders missing, defeat was inevitable.

Cradley were still without Irons when bottom-of-the-table Poole visited Dudley Wood, but with Craven returning, an easy win was on the cards. The Pirates had other ideas, however, and made their intentions clear as early as the first heat, when skipper Joe Bowkiss equalled the track record. The Cubs went into the last heat two points down, needing a 5-1 in the final race to take the match. With Hunt and Clifton leading the race, Cradley looked to have two more points in the bag, but Hunt's machine ground to a halt and Clifton's tyre burst, leaving Poole to win the race 5-1 and take the match! It was the Cubs' first and only home defeat in 1948.

Cradley Heath had made it plain that they would welcome promotion to the Second Division, and another Challenge match was arranged against Sheffield at the start of August at Dudley Wood. Even though the Tigers were without star rider Bruce Semmens, Cradley elected to use Middlesbrough's Dick Tolley as a guest as Craven had now joined Wright and Irons on the injured list. He scored an immaculate maximum and led the Cubs to an 8-point victory.

Due to their injury problems, Cradley were allowed to sign Ken Sharples on loan from Belle Vue. He scored 3 points on his debut at Southampton, but the Cubs were no match for the Saints and lost heavily, 25-58. Approximately 400 supporters made the trip to Banister Court and joined the riders at the Speedway Sportsdome for dinner and dancing after the match.

Cradley had no vacant date in which to fit their first leg of the North v. South Cup (N/S Cup) and had to settle for riding the fixture at the neutral Sun Street Stadium against Tamworth. With Hunt having a quiet match, the Cubs were poor opposition for the Hounds and faced the second leg at Fazeley with a 20-point deficit to overcome.

Tamworth were again Cradley's next opponents at Dudley Wood, this time in the League, and once more, the Hounds refused to 'heel', snatching a draw in the last heat. This incredible match saw the return of Gil Craven, whose maximum was spoilt only by a misunderstanding between him and Phil Malpass, allowing Bill Dalton to cross the line in a dead heat with Gil. Alan Hunt, after a bad start, was awarded 2 points in the last race when, having been fenced by Basil Harris, he somersaulted over the finishing line. Harris was excluded for dangerous riding. A few nights later, the great rivals met at Fazeley for the second leg of the N/S Cup, with Eric Irons making his return. Cradley put up a hell of a fight, but a 3-point defeat on the night meant that Tamworth had put them out of the Cup competition in the first round.

Back in League action at Dudley Wood and with the team at full strength (Wright excluded), Cradley made short work of Poole and Hull before embarking on one of their ill-fated southern coast tours. A heavy defeat at Poole was followed by the inevitable thrashing at Southampton, but the following week saw the Cubs emerge with some credit by beating Yarmouth at Caister Road. Cradley featured their new rider, Bill Kemp, signed on loan from Wembley. He made an impressive debut, pairing up with skipper Beaumont to score 6 points, but the star of the night was Alan Hunt, who burst back into form, dropping just a single point to Bloaters skipper Reg Morgan.

September continued with victories over Exeter and Hanley at Dudley Wood, and the matches saw the formation of the Hunt/Irons pairing that was to become one of the most prolific in the League. After losing at Hull, Cradley moved into top gear. With Irons, Hunt, Craven, Beaumont and Kemp all riding well, they won at Hanley and dispatched Coventry and Yarmouth from Dudley Wood with ease. Coventry were again unsuccessful visitors at the beginning of October, as were the formidable Southampton, although the omnipotent Alf Bottoms was unbeaten and also took a whole second off the track record in the first heat. But just as Cradley were beginning to have that Championship look about them, disaster struck in the second half of the meeting. Craven fell, chipping a bone in the base of his spine – his season was over.

The Cubs refused to be denied so late in the season, and kept up the pressure with a win at Wombwell, but despite a maximum from Hunt, they failed at Coventry. When Cradley lost their next match at Plymouth, it effectively ended their chances of winning the League, but they were determined to take second place and hammered Hastings at Dudley Wood.

A win at Tamworth would secure that second spot. Ken Sharples saved up his best performance of the season and, along with Hunt, scored a maximum as Cradley walloped the Hounds and won the match by 22 points.

Cradley finished the season in style at Dudley Wood with a record League win over Wombwell 66-18. They had once again finished as runners-up, this time to Exeter, leaving Southampton and Tamworth in their wake.

The Cubs at full strength had been a formidable outfit, and in Gil Craven they had one of the surprise successes of the season, Gil topping Cradley's averages with 8.75 points, just ahead of Les Beaumont. Eric Irons also exceeded the 8-point average, and he was followed closely by the unfortunate Jimmy Wright. Alan Hunt would no doubt have improved on his 7.21 average if not for the fact that he had suffered more than his share of machine problems. Even so, he remained one of the most exciting riders in the division. For the first time since the war, promotion and relegation was introduced and with four teams due to be promoted, Cradley were on their way into the Second Division.

3

THE HEATHENS
1949

There had been movement in the Cradley camp during the winter months, in prepa-
ration for their debut in the Second Division. A training school had produced a
likely looking pair of youngsters in Les Tolley and Jim Pain, but a shock came when Eric
Irons announced his retirement.

More riders left as Ken Sharples returned to his parent club, Belle Vue, and Jimmy
Wright, still not fully recovered from his terrible injuries sustained at Exeter, was loaned
out to Oxford. Promoter Les Marshall relinquished his interests at Cradley to concen-
trate on Birmingham, who had been promoted to the First Division, and Dudley
Marchant became the new team manager at Dudley Wood.

The Cradley management, however, had not been idle in the winter and had bought
Geoff Godwin from Newcastle, and had obtained Eric Williams on loan from Wembley
and Jack Arnfield from Harringay. A well-equipped workshop was set up at Dudley
Wood, and Bill Spencer, the chief mechanic at Birmingham, was appointed to take
charge of operations.

Phil Malpass was out of action even before the first match when he collided with Bill
Kemp in the pre-season practice and broke a bone in his hand. The Dudley Wood gates
opened on 1 April with a challenge match against Sheffield. Already without Malpass,
the Cubs were also without a further two riders as Arnfield and Craven had not yet
arrived from Australia and New Zealand. The loss proved too great as the Tigers, in
front of a 13,000-strong crowd, won by 14 points. The Cradley scorers were as follows:
Hunt (11), Les Beaumont (9), Ray Beaumont (4), Clifton (3), Godwin (3), Williams (2),
Kemp (2), Wilstead (0).

One week later, Cradley began their League campaign with a match against another
team new to the division, visitors Walthamstow. The Cubs replaced Wilf Wilstead with
Roy Moreton, and the youngster was unbeaten by the opposition all night. Alan Hunt
scored a maximum and led Cradley to a 52-32 win. Hunt was again unbeaten the
following week when the Cubs beat Fleetwood at home by 16 points, Les Beaumont
and Moreton giving excellent support.

Cradley had their first setback when a strong Bristol team came to Dudley Wood and
put on a display of gating reckoned by the 15,000-strong crowd to be the best they had
ever seen. The superb Bill Hole and Jack Mountford gave an ominous warning of the
class of rider that Cradley were due to face in the Second Division, both remaining
unbeaten as Bristol stormed to a 50-34 win.

1949 programme cover.

Paddy Mills was one such rider, and when Norwich visited Cradley, he would have been unbeaten but for an engine failure. Although the Stars battled hard, the Cubs won the match thanks to 11 points from Roy Moreton, who had not been able to get a team place a few weeks earlier.

With Arnfield and Craven still on a ship sailing from the other side of the world, Cradley made their first away appearance at Edinburgh and were unlucky not to win. They were 8 points in front after six heats, but the Monarchs hit back, to take the lead and win the match by 4 points.

The Cubs remained in the north to take on Newcastle, but were completely outclassed and lost by almost 40 points, Hunt top-scoring for Cradley with a mere 5 points. Jim Pain was being given a run at reserve, but was finding it hard to score points.

The last match in April saw the Cubs able to field their full team for the first time that season as both Craven and Arnfield arrived. Les Beaumont was paired with Craven, Roy Moreton partnered Arnfield, and Eric Williams teamed up with Hunt to form an unbeaten paring in their debut at Dudley Wood against Southampton. The Saints were now without Alf Bottoms and although Beaumont took a nasty spill in his first race causing him to miss his next two, Cradley were comfortable winners. The overseas boys had quiet debuts and the star of the night was the likeable 'Whacker' Hunt, who scored a maximum and was beginning to prove that he was quite at home in this class of company.

May began with a defeat at Fleetwood and a win at home against Glasgow, but a visit to Norwich proved to be a costly affair with Hunt suffering machine failures and Arnfield and Williams damaging their bikes in other incidents, resulting in a huge defeat.

At Walthamstow, Les Beaumont was carried off on a stretcher after injuring his knee in the first race, but the Cubs battled valiantly and only lost the match in the final heat. It was bad news for Les however – he was out of the saddle for the next ten weeks.

Phil Malpass returned to the side and Hunt was made skipper for the visit of Coventry Bees. Although the new captain was bottom scorer, he still managed 5 points in an impressive all-round performance as Cradley completely swamped the Bees.

After losing at Ashfield, Cradley invited First Division Odsal to Dudley Wood for a challenge match. In front of 15,000 fans, some of the Cradley riders seemed somewhat overawed by the reputations of their opponents. Not so Alan Hunt. He passed Jack Biggs and then went around Ron Clarke on the last bend of the first race to claim a new track record of 73.2 seconds – shaving almost 1.5 seconds off the old record! However, Odsal always had the edge and were comfortable winners, 49-35. Hunt revelled in the top-class opposition and carried on 'revelling' the next day when he went to Rayleigh, won the Riders' Championship, and broke the track record into the bargain.

His partnership with Eric Williams was gaining a fearsome reputation, and they were unbeaten at Southampton as Cradley gained their first away win of the season. The Cubs concluded May by beating Newcastle at Dudley Wood on a miserable night, drizzling rain falling throughout the match. However, the awful conditions failed to prevent Hunt from scoring a maximum, and Moreton and Arnfield both recorded their first maximums for the club.

Arnfield had settled down more quickly than Gil Craven, who had not yet found his superb form of 1948. Jack's 10 points were instrumental in Cradley's 4-point win over Glasgow Ashfield at Dudley Wood in the first leg of the National Trophy. Ashfield arrived boasting the formidable Ken LeBreton, who had an awesome reputation, but he met his match in Alan Hunt, who scorched to a brilliant 18-point maximum and established himself as one of the top riders in the Second Division.

Falls by Hunt, Williams, Godwin and Craven cost the Cubs the match against Coventry, and their home fixture once again pitted them against First Division opposition, this time in the form of West Ham. Hunt, scoring 9 points, led Cradley to a fine 47-37 win, but Roy Moreton, having had a great match, was put into the fence by George Wilkes and somersaulted over the line with his bike on top of him, sustaining facial injuries that caused him to miss the next few matches.

When Cradley went to Ashfield for the second leg of the National Trophy, their 4-point lead frankly did not seem enough, but an absolutely superb team performance saw the Cubs win the away leg by 2 points and thus progress into the second round.

The middle of June saw Craven recover his form and win the £30 cheque when he top-scored in Cradley's round of the World Championship, and at Glasgow's White City he was the only rider to give Hunt any support as the Cubs crashed 30-54.

Cradley suffered a crushing 64-18 defeat at Fleetwood and complained to the Control Board that the track was unfit (as did the Fleetwood riders). There were only two riders who did not fall during the match, but in spite of this Eric Williams equalled the track record!

Geoff Godwin had arrived at Cradley Heath with a tremendous reputation, having won two Championship medals in the last three years. Since his arrival, his form had hardly been sensational, but he found it against visiting side Edinburgh, scoring 11 points along with Craven to lead the Cubs to an easy win.

Moreton returned to score a brilliant maximum at Coventry and, with Hunt and Arnfield scoring well, Cradley took two valuable League points off their local rivals.

The Cubs made life in the National Trophy difficult when they lost by 25 points in the first leg of the second round at Walthamstow, and further League points were dropped when they failed at Southampton.

The second leg of the National Trophy at Dudley Wood was reckoned to be one of the most exciting matches ever seen at Cradley. The Cubs had pulled back the deficit and led by a point going into the last heat. Walthamstow's Charlie May gated in front, but was closely followed by Jack Arnfield, who attempted to pass him coming out of the first bend. However, in doing so he fell, leaving May with a clear lead over Eric Williams, and with Benny King in third place it looked like a 4-2 heat win to the visitors, giving them a 1-point aggregate win. On the second lap King's engine blew, resulting in a 105-105 aggregate draw and a replay.

An easy win over Coventry at Dudley Wood proved to be costly for Cradley. Geoff Godwin fell in heat four and was hit by Bill Clifton, sustaining injuries that kept him out of speedway for three months. The pairing of Arnfield and Williams was a revelation however, taking 20 points out of a possible 21. Bristol were the favourites for the

1949 team line-up. From left to right, back row: Les Beaumont, Jack Arnfield, Bill Clifton, Roy Moreton. Front row: Eric Williams, Alan Hunt, Phil Malpass, Gil Craven.

Second Division title and boasted the best rider in the division in Billy Hole. When Cradley paid them a visit in early July, the Cubs failed to win a single heat at Knowle Stadium. Alan Hunt arrived with 'ANDY' written in big black letters on his fuel tank to celebrate the birth of his son. It was the only thing that Cradley had cause to celebrate on that particular day as they were hammered 62-22.

A busy month continued with the National Trophy replay at Walthamstow. A determined finish by the Londoners saw them 18 points up after the first leg. Jack Arnfield, who was being watched by the Australian Test selectors, was superb and would have scored an 18-point maximum but for a fall in his last race. Hunt also had an eventful night. After shedding a chain in his second ride, he was lapped just inches from the line as he attempted to push his bike home – and fainted! In a subsequent race, he locked bikes with Harry Edwards and both swerved on to the centre green, scattering the officials in all directions!

In the return at Dudley Wood a few nights later, both Hunt and Arnfield were unbeaten in their six outings to lead Cradley to a 71-37 win, putting the matter beyond any doubt and booking their place in the third round.

At Sheffield, Cradley lost Eric Williams when he fell in his first outing, and the Tigers took full advantage of Cradley's plight, winning 50-34. When Godwin had been injured, the Cubs had brought in young Les Tolley and, after a very shaky start, he was beginning to net a few points. The Cubs had never been a very popular nickname, so Alan Hunt and the rest of the team got together and decided that they should be known as the Heathens, which they were from mid-July.

Les Beaumont made his return as the Heathens welcomed Norwich in the third round of the National Trophy. He found the pace a little hot and scored only 3 points, but brilliant displays from Hunt and Arnfield assured Cradley of a 26-point lead to take into the second leg. In the event it was not enough and Norwich reached their third National Trophy Final in as many years with a scintillating display that saw them win on aggregate in the very last race.

When Edinburgh visited Dudley Wood, they brought with them future World Champion Jack Young, but even he could not live with the Arnfield/Williams pairing who romped through the meeting unbeaten, leading the Heathens to an easy win. Roy Moreton, after asking for a transfer, was left out of the team.

Ashfield were a 'colourful' side who included a trio of Aussies as their heat-leaders. There was Ken LeBreton – the White Ghost; Merv Harding – the Red Shadow; and Keith Gurtner – the Blue Devil. Indeed, Ashfield's line-up read more like a Dulux colour chart rather than a speedway team, but they put up a spirited show at Cradley, losing by only 12 points in what was a thrilling match. Hunt was again too good for the Aussies.

Cradley's first fixture in August attracted a record crowd of 24,000 spectators to Dudley Wood. The occasion was a challenge match against First Division neighbours Birmingham, but it was a disappointing affair with Hunt not providing the expected heroics and the rest of the team generally 'off the boil'. The Brummies proved to be a far superior team and won the match comfortably, 51-32. Eric Williams was the only Heathen to beat Graham Warren.

Southampton were uninspired visitors in Cradley's next match and were dispatched without much ado, but the same could be said of The Heathens' performance at Edinburgh, where they failed to put up any opposition.

Following a challenge match between a combined Oxford and Coventry side against Cradley at Cowley, which the Heathens won, negotiations were completed for the transfer of Roy Moreton to Coventry for a reported fee of £600. Craven was injured in the match and missed Cradley's next two fixtures.

Reserves Pain and Tolley were outstanding at Dudley Wood, and made up for Craven's absence as Cradley outclassed Newcastle. After the match, Hunt beat First Division Wimbledon's Norman Parker 2-0 in a special match race, suggesting that he would probably be at home in top division company.

He top-scored for the Heathens at Walthamstow, but received such scant support that Cradley lost by 24 points. Hunt followed that performance by scoring a paid maximum at Dudley Wood, leading the Heathens to a 4-point win over Fleetwood. The visitors received many gift points after falls by Malpass and Craven (twice) and engine failures by Arnfield and Williams.

Towards the end of August, Cradley visited second-placed Sheffield, who were considered to be almost invincible at Owlerton. The Heathens gave the Tigers plenty to think about, but with Gil Craven still not fully fit and failing to score, the task was too great and Cradley eventually lost by 49-35. The following night found the Tigers at Dudley Wood, and swift revenge was gained as the Heathens turned on the heat with maximums for Hunt, Arnfield and Williams. Alan set the scene when he broke his own track record in heat one, recording a time of 72.8 seconds.

Geoff Godwin.

Les Beaumont, Cradley's first skipper.

Hunt continued to be the scourge of the Second Division, scoring a maximum at Newcastle and beating England stars Dent Oliver and Louis Lawson in the second half of the meeting, but a machine failure by Arnfield when he was leading the last race cost Cradley the match by a single point.

After losing a further match at Glasgow White City, the Heathens returned home to thrash Norwich. Phil Malpass scored his first ever maximum, but it was Eric Williams' turn to take the limelight on this particular night, as he beat Aussie Test star Aub Lawson 2-0 in a special match race in the second half.

Malpass was still in the mood the very next night at Perry Barr, when the Heathens challenged First Division Birmingham. Despite a fall, he top-scored for Cradley, but Eric Williams, after a fall in his second race, retired from the meeting. The Heathens struggled without him and could only muster 28 points against their superior neighbours.

Eric was back in the saddle the following week at Cradley and celebrated with a maximum. With Hunt and Craven joining him and Malpass continuing his purple patch, visitors Glasgow only managed to score 25 points.

In mid-September, the Heathens faced a daunting task at Knowle Stadium where they faced League leaders Bristol, and although their 31-53 defeat did not reflect it, they pushed the Bulldogs all the way in the best match at Bristol all season. This was reflected at the end of the match when the Bristol team manager went out onto the track and asked for three cheers for the Cradley team.

Sheffield and Ashfield gave little resistance at Dudley Wood, with Hunt, Arnfield, Williams and Craven all riding brilliantly, and with Malpass and Beaumont filling in the middle scores, Cradley were easy winners of both matches.

Newly crowned League Champions Bristol were the next visitors to the Black Country circuit, but even they could only muster 30 points, as the Heathens ran riot. Bulldogs skipper and the Second Division's top scorer Billy Hole managed to score only 7 points.

The following evening, Cradley remained 'on song' at Glasgow and beat Ashfield, thanks to Hunt and Williams. Alan was beaten only by Ken LeBreton, but gained his revenge in a subsequent heat. However, the match marked the end of the season for Jack Arnfield, who was injured sufficiently to miss the last five matches.

Jim Pain was brought in at Fleetwood but failed to score, as Cradley lost by 10 points. The highlight of the match was an amazing heat seven crash when Les Tolley tangled with Peter Orpwood and fell. However, his machine carried on, climbed the fence and finally hooked itself on the end of a pylon where it performed all manner of gyrations until the motor was turned off. When Tolley was mounted on the machine for the remainder of the season, it must also have 'recharged' him. He scored 8 points at Dudley Wood as Cradley murdered Walthamstow, and he followed this with 7 points against unsuccessful visitors Coventry, but to top it all in the return at Brandon, he scored a marvellous maximum as the Heathens romped to a massive win.

The last meeting of the season at Dudley Wood was the Adams Trophy which was won appropriately by Alan Hunt, but Cradley had saved the best till last when they completed their fixtures by winning at third-placed Norwich. Even without Arnfield they rode to a fabulous two-point win thanks to immaculate performances by Williams, Craven and Hunt. It secured fourth place in the League for the Heathens behind Bristol, Sheffield and Norwich.

Cradley had reason to be proud of their performance in their first year in the Second Division. Hunt had been tremendous, finishing the year with a 9.16 average, and the only rider in the division to score a higher points average was Billy Hole. The First Division riders were all eyeing him up as a definite future opponent.

Eric Williams, after a slow start, also had a splendid season, rattling off maximums and being much better than his 7.5 point average suggested. Gil Craven also suffered from a slow start and together with an injury, he saw his average slip to 6.51, but the end of the season had seen the Craven of old. Jack Arnfield had been a success. He went through a purple patch in mid-season that saw him score just as prolifically as Hunt, but early season inconsistency kept his average down to 6.13 points.

An injury to Les Beaumont saw him struggle for much of the season, and Les finished with his lowest ever average for the Heathens of 4.16 points. Phil Malpass had shown flashes of brilliance, and the end of the season saw him as a much more consistent rider, but an indifferent start to the season kept his average as low as 4.06 points. Geoff Godwin rode in only 21 matches, averaging 4.47 points, and frankly did not live up to expectations, whereas young Les Tolley exceeded his, finishing the year brilliantly. Roy Moreton, after a promising start, had been transferred to Coventry, but there had been other departees too. Bill Kemp failed to make the grade and was transferred to Oxford, Wilf Wilstead joined Birmingham and Ray Beaumont was loaned to Tamworth.

4

HUNT'S LAST STAND
1950

An icy wind blew through speedway in 1950 as crowds dropped by twenty per cent, with the draught being felt particularly by the London tracks. The basic reason for this was that a lot more counter-attractions were on offer. One notable example was that motoring made considerable headway as petrol was de-rationed in May. It should also be mentioned that the weather in 1950 was awful.

The Second Division lost Bristol and gained Yarmouth, Halifax, Hanley and Plymouth, and the Shield competition was introduced as a warm-up to the League fixtures. Cradley retained the squad of 1949 apart from Eric Williams, who was recalled to Wembley.

Craven was again a late arrival, so for the opening challenge match against the 'North' at Dudley Wood, the Heathens called up a youngster from Alan Hunt's winter training school – Harry Bastable. He showed promise, scoring 3 points, but despite a maximum from Hunt, Cradley lost their opener by 2 points.

Craven arrived a week later to line up against Coventry in the first match of the South Shield campaign, and with the Heathens at full strength, the Bees were beaten $57\frac{1}{2}$ - $26\frac{1}{2}$. Cradley's scorers were as follows: Alan Hunt ($11\frac{1}{2}$), Les Tolley (11), Phil Malpass (9), Gil Craven (8), Jack Arnfield (7), Bill Clifton (5), Les Beaumont (4), Jim Pain (2).

A new concrete starting pad had been laid at Dudley Wood and it was of some concern to Hunt. Upon the visit of Plymouth, he was last from the tapes in all of his rides, only to come from the back to score a maximum. Tolley and Craven gave him solid support and the Heathens won the match by 10 points.

Defeats followed at Coventry and Southampton. At Banister Road, Craven injured an ankle in his third outing, causing him to retire from the meeting. Les Beaumont, after a poor start to the season, was rested. Geoff Godwin was brought in at Plymouth and even though he scored only 2 points, Cradley put up a fine show and took 2 Shield points away from the Devils.

Bastable found himself back in the team as the Heathens played host to Norwich in a thrilling match that Cradley won in the last heat, but only 3,000 fans braved the snow and wintry conditions to see Hunt lower the track record to 72.2 seconds and help himself to another maximum.

At the end of April, Yarmouth supplied the first rider to beat Hunt at Dudley Wood in 1950 – Billy Bales. The nineteen-year-old equalled the track record in doing so, and

1950 programme cover.

beat Alan once more in the final heat, but his efforts were not enough to save the Bloaters, and Cradley won the match 49-35. For the Heathens' trip to Norwich, Beaumont returned and Frank Young was given a chance at reserve, and once again Cradley got the better of the Stars. Hunt dropped just a point in the match and before-hand he beat Phil Clarke 2-0 in the first leg of the Silver Helmet.

Bastable once again found his services required at Dudley Wood when Southampton took Cradley all the way, only to be beaten in the last heat. It was, however, the following week that Harry shone in a match against Walthamstow. Craven and Arnfield both crashed in the match and were taken to hospital but, despite this, the Heathens soldiered on and, with Harry scoring 7 points, Hunt 11, Malpass 10 and Tolley 9, Cradley found enough in reserve to win the match 49-35.

In the return encounter two nights later, Cradley were still without Arnfield and had a vulnerable tail-end in Bastable, Pain, Clifton and Young, and with only 4 points forth-coming from these four, the result was an inevitable thrashing.

Cradley's next fixture was a challenge match at Dudley Wood against the mighty First Division Wembley, who were without the super Tommy Price. Alan Hunt sent the crowd wild before the match by beating Phil Clarke 2-0 to win the Silver Helmet and then promptly asking for a transfer! His place in the Cradley side was taken by Bastable, and Dennis Newton was drafted in at reserve. Predictably, the Lions won easily, but the match marked the emergence of Frank Young, who beat Bill Kitchen to gain his first ever race win for the Heathens.

Just one week later at Cradley, Frank scored a brilliant 16 points against Ashfield in the first leg of the National Trophy. Arnfield made his comeback only to get injured again, but with Gil Craven taking over from Hunt as skipper and dropping a solitary point, the Heathens established a 13-point lead.

The following evening, Ashfield, led by LeBreton, scored a 14-point win and put Cradley out of the competition. Johnnie Hoskins, the Glasgow promoter, said: 'Cradley made me a gift of this match by omitting Hunt. He was the only serious obstacle in our chance of survival.' Johnnie had apparently overlooked the 12 and 10 points scored by Craven and Young respectively, as well as the absence of Arnfield –at the end of the day, Ashfield had won by only 1 point, not 51!

At the end of May, Cradley agreed to transfer Hunt to Harringay for £2,500, but at a Control Board investigation on 2 June, the rider elected to stay at Cradley. On the same day, Les Marshall once again took over at Cradley Heath.

By the time Cradley's next match came around on 5 June, Hunt's transfer contro-versy had been settled and he rejoined the Heathens at Dudley Wood to beat the living daylights out of Edinburgh. However, the Monarchs did boast the star of the night in Australian Jack Young, who took away Hunt's only point, and was unbeaten all night. Arnfield returned to score 5 points.

Although Cradley lost their next match at Yarmouth, they scored enough points to win the Kemsley South Shield from nearest rivals Coventry, thanks to Hunt and Young. A narrow defeat at Edinburgh marked the Heathens debut in the League, and although Hunt dropped a point to Jack Young, he gained his revenge in the last heat of the match. Cradley then embarked on a series of challenge matches at Dudley Wood, the first being against a London Select side made up of riders from First Division Harringay and New Cross. To add a little parity to proceedings, Graham Warren was brought into the Heathens side as a guest and dropped only 1 point as he lead the Black Country side to a 46-38 win.

Warren was on the opposing team when Cradley took on the Kangaroos, and although he scored an 18-point maximum, he could not prevent a 60-48 win for the Heathens. Cradley's guest on this occasion was the legendary Jack Parker, who scored 11 points. Alan Hunt opened proceedings by beating Ken LeBreton 2-0 in the Silver Helmet match race championship.

The last challengers were Birmingham and, even without Warren and Arthur Payne, the Brummies were too good for Cradley, winning the match 47-37. They were not too good for Alan Hunt, however, who sailed through the match unbeaten and lowered the track record to 72.0 seconds. Hunt was well and truly back, much to the relief of the fans, but as one door opened, another one closed and Jack Arnfield was injured and out of the sport for two months.

The beginning of July welcomed Coventry to Dudley Wood in a League match. Cradley's tail end, once again looked suspect with Bastable, Bill Clifton and Geoff Newman filling in. This would have been all very well if all the other riders had performed, but they didn't. Craven and Young never got going and the Bees took full advantage, winning the match by 2 points.

The fans demanded urgent action, and the management reciprocated as twenty-three-year-old Yorkshireman Eric Boothroyd and London-born Brian Shepherd were signed from Third Division Tamworth. Both did well on their debut at Dudley Wood, scoring 10 and 7 points respectively as the Heathens beat Newcastle. With Hunt and Craven away on World Championship duty, Malpass and Tolley held the team together, but Frank Young's form had dipped badly and never again would he recapture the rich vein of scoring that he enjoyed just a few short weeks before.

At Newcastle, only Hunt and Tolley performed and the Heathens lost convincingly. They fared no better at White City when they were there without Hunt, who was riding for England against Australia at New Cross. Alan scored 7 points on his international debut, and in his other two appearances in the Test Series, he scored 12 at Wimbledon and 5 at Wembley. He was a revelation riding against the best riders from the First Division, and it was testimony to Alan's reputation that he had become the first ever Second Division rider to be selected to ride in a Test Series.

Realistically, however, the writing was on the wall regarding Whacker's future at Dudley Wood. He was obviously a man destined to make it to the very top in speedway – and Second Division racing was not going to take him there.

Halifax were Cradley's next visitors in the middle of July and arrived at Dudley Wood with an unbeaten League record. Their ace card was eighteen-year-old Arthur Forrest, who put on a superb display, being beaten only by Hunt who equalled the track record in doing so, but the Heathens' all-round strength made them the masters by 14 points.

Hunt was the only performing Heathen as Cradley lost heavily at Walthamstow, but he was strangely subdued at Halifax where Eric Boothroyd took over the reins to keep them in a match that was eventually lost by 10 points.

The Heathens' next matches were in the Midland Cup against a much-improved Coventry side. At Brandon on Bank Holiday Monday morning, Cradley forced a draw, but the night return at Dudley Wood saw the lead change hands six times before the Heathens finally won the match by 7 points and lifted the Cup.

After winning at Sheffield, Cradley had a shock when visiting Plymouth came and gave them a 56-28 thrashing in a disastrous match at Dudley Wood. Malpass and Tolley were unfit to ride, and Arnfield stepped back into the side but it was the Heathens' worst home performance to date.

The same sort of result looked on the cards the following week at Cradley, as Hanley won the first three heats, but the Heathens' youngest pairing of Boothroyd and Shepherd inspired a fighting comeback to ensure victory.

Defeats at Coventry and Norwich followed, and after the Brandon match, Jack Arnfield, who had had a miserable season, returned to Australia. His place was taken by Laurie Schofield from Tamworth, who scored 3 points on his debut at Norwich.

Although Hunt was on World Championship duty at Wimbledon, double-figure scores from Malpass, Craven and Boothroyd ensured success against White City at Dudley Wood.

A visit to Fleetwood netted the Heathens another 2 League points. The Fliers were without the injured Dick Geary and when they came to Dudley Wood a few nights later, they were unmercifully hammered 58-26 in front of Cradley's lowest ever crowd of

Jimmy Wright.

Alan Hunt.

Jack Arnfield.

1,500 people. Brian Shepherd was proving to be an inspired signing, and he led the pack with 11 points as Cradley won by 50-34 at Hanley with a brilliant team performance.

The Heathens began to climb up the League table after a boring slaughter of Yarmouth at Dudley Wood and took the points in the return at Caister Road the following evening in the Bloaters' first home defeat since April.

Shepherd recorded his first maximum when Southampton were unsuccessful visitors to Dudley Wood, despite Cradley losing Craven with an ankle injury. In the return at Banister Road, however, only Hunt scored well, and dropped his only point to Saints' skipper Jimmy Squibb as the Heathens lost 52-31.

Undaunted, Cradley carried on to Plymouth and won by 4 points with an impressive team performance that put them in third place in the League – 7 points behind leaders Norwich with two matches in hand.

In fact, Norwich were the next visitors to Dudley Wood at the beginning of October, and Cradley kept up the pressure on the Stars by easily winning the match. The scorers were as follows: Hunt (12), Craven (11), Boothroyd (9), Shepherd (9), Tolley (6), Malpass (5), Clifton (3) and Schofield (2).

Cradley finished off the season in style, beating Ashfield home and away and taking the points against Walthamstow and Sheffield; Hunt dropped just one point in all four matches. However, although they finished just 1 point behind Champions Norwich, the Heathens were relegated to third position by White City who had scored more match points. But for losing at home against Coventry and Plymouth, Cradley would have been champions.

It had, however, been a satisfactory season. Hunt had grown in stature, and was now in fact too big for the team. He averaged 10.04 points, but with every First Division promoter knocking on his door, his continued presence at Dudley Wood looked to be in doubt.

Eric Boothroyd and Brain Shepherd had been shrewd signings, both averaging 6.5 points, and the ever-enthusiastic Phil Malpass was not far behind them. Gil Craven had had a poor year by his own standards, averaging just under 6 points in a season that had seen him dogged by injuries, and young Les Tolley was hot on his heels with 5.85 points.

Laurie Schofield, although averaging only 3.83 points, had finished the season with a flourish, scoring 11 points in the final match, and looked to be a good bet for the future, as did Harry Bastable, who had featured in the early part of the season. At one point, Frank Young looked to be the find of the season, but he 'blew up' and was even unable to keep his place in the team. Frank averaged 3.4 points.

Ever faithful Bill Clifton averaged 3.34 points, but poor old Jack Arnfield, who had had a nightmare season, found himself on a 2.8 point average before he packed up and went home to lick his many wounds. In the close season, the Cradley supporters received the expected 'kick in the teeth' – Alan Hunt had been signed by Birmingham. Cradley Heathens had lost their favourite son.

5

THE DECLINE BEGINS
1951

Thirty-seven teams were due to contest the 1951 League programme but the decline of speedway continued and Southampton and Sheffield fell by the wayside after a few weeks. Something near panic set in as the season progressed, with the usual subjects of pay-rates and entertainment tax looming large. Birmingham dealt Cradley a further blow when they signed Eric Boothroyd and thus boasted the two top Heathens from the 1950 season. Craven, Tolley, Shepherd, Malpass and Schofield had all been retained, Dick Tolley (Les's brother) and Dennis Hitchings had been signed, and Harry Bastable had been bought in 'full-time' to complete the squad. Wilf Wilstead and Bill Clifton remained as 'back-up'.

The Heathens got off to the best possible start when they won at Liverpool in a Central Shield match. For their opener, Cradley invited the mighty Brummies to Dudley Wood, who even without injured Graham Warren thrashed the Heathens 54-24. The irony was that Birmingham's top scorers were all ex-Heathens. Hunt and Boothroyd rubbed salt in the wound by scoring maximums and Geoff Bennett scored 11 points.

The Central Shield competition continued as new skipper Gil Craven and Brian Shepherd led Cradley to a win at Dudley Wood over Hanley, before losing the return at Stoke. Les Beaumont, who had been 'surplus to requirements', had found himself a home at promoted Leicester, and he made a triumphant return to Dudley Wood, scoring 8 points as the Hunters scored an upset by winning the match 46-38, and they repeated the dose back at their own track.

At this early stage of the season, the Heathens were an inconsistent bunch, Shepherd and the vastly improved Laurie Schofield being the best of them. Indeed, in Cradley's best performance of the year so far at Dudley Wood, Laurie's clash with the brilliant unbeaten Arthur Forest was the highlight of the night as the Heathens caned Halifax. Further Shield points were taken at Sheffield, as the Tigers found themselves without star rider Len Williams, and Cradley were back in contention for Central Shield honours.

During the next few days, Dudley Wood was graced by two riders who were to become 'all-time greats' of the sport. Towards the end of April, Cradley staged a challenge match between the Midlands and the Kangaroos. Nineteen-year-old Ronnie Moore dropped just a point for the 'Roos in his debut at Dudley Wood, when he was beaten by the opposition's Norman Parker, who was his captain at Wimbledon.

Cradley ended the month with a remarkable match at Halifax. The first ten heats were all drawn, with Halifax riders winning them all and Heathens in second and third places. A Cradley rally followed with Schofield settling the issue in the last heat by beating Jack Hughes to give the Heathens a 43-41 win. Harry Bastable, meanwhile, was making slow but sure progress, and when a poor Sheffield side visited Cradley, Harry scored 8 points from reserve and clocked the fastest time of the season with 73.4 seconds. It was Sheffield's last match before disbanding.

The next match at Dudley Wood saw the Cradley debut of the second 'all-time great'. When the Heathens overwhelmed Liverpool to win the Central Shield, the visitors had a certain Peter Craven at reserve, who showed little of the form that later led him to be World Champion when he failed to score. New boy Dick Tolley was superb and had hit a rich vein of form, which was just as well as Shepherd fell in the match and broke his leg.

The Heathens began their League campaign at Dudley Wood by beating Southampton, but the result was struck from the record when the Saints subsequently withdrew from the League. With Shepherd sidelined for some time, Cradley signed Guy Allott from the defunct Sheffield, and he made his debut at Dudley Wood, scoring 10 points as the Heathens beat Oxford. The visitors were no match for Cradley, but interest was kept alive mainly by ex-Heathens Eric Irons and Bill Kemp who between them scored half of Oxford's 28 points.

Coventry were Cradley's opponents in the first round of the National Trophy and at Brandon, superbly led by Schofield and Craven, the Heathens established a 12-point lead on which they built a few days later at Dudley Wood to put their local rivals out of the competition.

Schofield had become the new 'darling' of the team, scoring an abundance of points at home and away, and Craven was currently riding on top form. Malpass, probably spurred on by the rapid improvement of Bastable, was settling to become a reliable solid scorer, and Guy Allott looked to be an adequate replacement for Shepherd. The Tolley brothers both showed flashes of brilliance, but their inconsistency prevented Cradley from boasting the best line-up in the Second Division at that time. Dennis Hitchings kept plugging away, never causing a sensation but always chipping in with points.

The Heathens' return to League racing, at Fleetwood, was costly. They lost Malpass in heat six when he crashed into the fence and severely mangled the little finger on his left hand as well as fracturing another digit, keeping him out of the team for three weeks. Despite a fighting display by Bastable that saw him top-score with 9 points, Cradley lost the match. Even without Malpass, the Heathens were too strong for Weymouth at Dudley Wood. Bill Clifton was recalled to the side, and the star of the night was the Bloaters' Fred Brand, who was never bothered by any of the home riders.

The Heathens continued their National Trophy campaign at Ashfield, and when Craven was badly shaken in the first heat after his handlebars snapped and sent him into the fence, Cradley's chances looked dubious. After missing a ride, Gil continued to score 4 valuable points, but a deficit of 34 points seemed a mountain to climb in the second leg at Dudley Wood. In the return leg six nights later, Cradley staged one of their greatest performances ever. They had made up the deficit by heat ten and moved into the semi-final of the National Trophy, beating Ashfield 83-25. The Heathens scorers were as follows: Les Tolley (15), Craven (15), Allott (14), Schofield (12), Dick Tolley (10), Bastable (7), Hitchings (6) and Clifton (4).

Malpass returned to Dudley Wood in mid-June and, although still suffering from his injuries, rode with great determination to score 9 points as the confident Heathens easily beat White City. Newcastle fared no better at Cradley, but on their own track they beat the Heathens by just 2 points in the final heat decider.

Cradley began to climb up the League table and when they beat Liverpool home and away, Allott being unbeaten in both matches, League honours looked a distinct possibility. First of all, however, they were due to face top-of-the-League Norwich in the National Trophy semi-final, in what was expected to be a titanic struggle. The first leg took place in early July at Norwich, and a 10,000-strong crowd were treated to the best racing seen all year at Firs Stadium. Cradley were 20 points down after seven heats, but fought back desperately through Craven and Schofield to end the match with a 27½-point deficit.

Two nights later in the return leg on a rain-soaked Dudley Wood circuit, the Stars were much sharper away from the tapes than the Heathens and with overtaking virtually impossible, Cradley lost the match 47-61 and crashed out of the competition at the final fence. Whether the defeat knocked the stuffing out of the Heathens is speculation, but it began a string of four defeats, beginning at Oxford and continuing at Leicester on Bank Holiday Monday morning. On the same evening, the Hunters rode at Dudley Wood in front of Cradley's lowest crowd ever and inflicted upon the Heathens their biggest home defeat to date when they won by 61-23. Les Beaumont was Leicester's top scorer in both matches. Further misery followed as a defeat at Yarmouth sent Cradley tumbling down the League table.

On 10 August, Cradley staged an England *v.* Scotland international, all riders being chosen from the Second Division. England won the match 61-47, led by Allott, Malpass and Craven, but the star of the night belonged to Scotland (Australia actually) as Edinburgh's Jack Young tore up the opposition to record an immaculate 18-point maximum. Just a few weeks later at Wembley, he was to become the first ever Second Division rider to become World Speedway Champion.

Meanwhile, back in the real world, Cradley received another body blow as Laurie Schofield was 'called up' by the RAF. Bill Clifton was brought in at Dudley Wood for a Midland Cup match against Hanley. The Heathens, with Craven, Allott and Bastable firing on all cylinders, took an 18-point advantage to Hanley. A great display by reserve Dick Tolley saw Cradley hold Hanley to a 5-point win at Stoke to win the leg on aggregate and progress into the next round.

Les Tolley had been rested and the young Australian Don Pettijohn was given a run at reserve, scoring 3 points at Dudley Wood as Fleetwood were dispatched with ease. But things were not so good in the Cradley camp as they went into September with promotional wrangles and riders unsettled. At one stage, racing was suspended for a short time but promoter Eli Sumner completed the season. However, a change of race night saw Cradley in direct competition with neighbouring Wolverhampton. The Cradley team spirit was in the doldrums, and the Heathens were unable to hold visiting

1951 programme cover.

Walthamstow. They were completely outclassed in the return at the London track, losing by a massive 21-63. A further blow followed when Craven announced that he had 'had enough' and returned to New Zealand. Phil Malpass was appointed captain but failed to boost flagging morale, as Halifax won at Cradley by 10 points. Les Tolley was recalled to the weakened squad, and only he and Malpass performed for the Heathens as an inevitable slaughter took place at Norwich.

Cradley's next match in the Midland Cup was at Birmingham and although Malpass scored a gritty 10 points, maximums from Hunt and Warren for the Brummies made them easy winners by 65-30. Cradley's manager Dick Wise resigned after the meeting. In the second leg, at Dudley Wood, Warren Hunt, Ron Mountford and Jim Tolley were all unbeaten for Birmingham, who won the match 62-34.

Back in league action, Ashfield were also successful visitors to Dudley Wood, but the Heathens scored their first win in seven matches over Coventry at Cradley to conclude a very black September. The return at Brandon saw Laurie Schofield on leave and back in Cradley colours, but he was sadly out of touch and score only 3 points as the Bees romped home 57-27. In the Heathens' next match, at Halifax, however, he looked more his old self, top-scoring with 9 points but it was not enough to save Cradley.

Phil Malpass had taken the captain's role to heart, and was not content to see the Heathens 'roll over and die'. He spurred them on at Motherwell, only to have victory snatched away from them in the final heat when the Lanarkshire team stole a 2-point win. Cradley were to have many years in their history when just as things appeared not

Gil Craven.

Bill Clifton.

to be able to get any worse, they did – 1951 was one of these years. In their next match at Hanley, Malpass crashed in heat four and broke his collarbone. Cradley lost the match by a country mile.

Bill Clifton had been granted a free transfer and the Heathens now faced a difficulty in fielding a full side. Wilf Wilstead and Don Pettijohn were brought in to make up a dreadfully weak-looking team, and on visits to Ashfield and White City, Cradley failed to net even 30 points. Back at Dudley Wood, Bastable took up the reins. He scored 9 points against Edinburgh but it was not enough to save the match and Wilstead crashed, leaving Cradley with only seven riders. Harry followed that with 10 points against visiting Norwich, but the result was the same – another loss.

Still only able to field seven riders, the Heathens rode their last away fixture at Edinburgh and scored only 23 points. Their final meeting of the season at Dudley Wood was a double-header on 19 October. Motherwell were the first opponents, and 10 points from Bastable allowed the Heathens to scrape home by just 2 points. However, they were not so lucky against Hanley, and Cradley lost their last match of the season by 20 points.

It had been a dire season for the Black Country team. They had finished fifteenth in a league of sixteen and had lost their favourite son the previous winter. Alan Hunt had gone on to rock the speedway world, and only Aub Lawson finished above him in the First Division scorers. Hunt had also reached his first World Championship final and had become an England regular. It seemed that as fast as his star was ascending, so Cradley's was descending.

The Heathens had lost Gil Craven, their star rider and skipper, in September and had lost his replacement, Phil Malpass, one month later. They had been robbed of star riders Shepherd and Schofield by injury and National Service and although Laurie had returned, the spark had gone. Craven had been the best of the bunch, averaging 8 points, with Malpass following him on 7. Allott, after a promising start, became wildly inconsistent and finished the season with an average of just over 6 points.

Les Tolley was just behind him. On some nights he was Cradley's top rider, but inconsistency cost him his team place for a while, and it was a problem that he never mastered in 1951. Harry Bastable finished the year with a mere 4.83 point average, but it belied his season. By the end of it, he was the rider that they were all talking about as he finished with a flourish that saw him as the Heathens top scorer in four out of the last five matches.

After a slow start, Laurie Schofield became arguably the best rider in the team, but a combination of conscription and a bout of bad form saw his average fall as low as 4.2 points. Dick Tolley was often a match-winner for Cradley, but inconsistency ran in the Tolleys' blood and Dick averaged only 4.2 points. Dennis Hitchings completed the Heathens' League averages with 2.32 points. As another season closed, the supporters walked through the Dudley Wood gates for the last time that year to make their way home and reflect on an awful season. The problem was that there weren't so many of them now, and thousands fewer than there had been only three years earlier.

6
DUDLEY WOOD CLOSES ITS DOORS
1952

The year 1952 saw the Second Division lose promoted Norwich and also Walthamstow, Halifax, Fleetwood and Newcastle who all failed to re-open. They did, however, welcome newly-promoted Poole, but these were grim days for speedway and the entertainment tax was lowered to twenty-five per cent enabling admission prices at the tracks to be reduced in an effort to increase attendances.

Eli Sumner bravely continued at Cradley Heath despite a loss of some £6,000 on the previous year. Money was still tight and the riders agreed to revert to the pay scales of 1950. This was not enough to entice Gil Craven back to the fold, but Cradley retained the services of Malpass, Bastable, Schofield, Shepherd, Allott and the Tolley brothers. In fact, they increased their number of Tolley brothers by signing Jim Tolley from Birmingham. Jim's Brummie team-mate Fred Perkins completed the 1952 Heathens squad.

They got off to a poor start at Oxford when Malpass' bike packed up after he had won his first race. With no track spares available, Cradley slumped to a 51-30 defeat. The Heathens then engaged in what was generally regarded as one of the greatest meetings ever seen at Blackbird Road as they just pipped Leicester in the last heat to win by 4 points. The result was reversed the following evening in Cradley's home debut, and this time it was the Hunters who were 44-40 winners. A new top surface had been laid on the track, and Bastable, who had top-scored for Cradley in the last two League matches, equalled Alan Hunt's track record in heat eleven.

In the Heathens' next home match, against Liverpool, Harry went one better, setting a new record of 71.4 seconds and completing the match with only 1 point dropped to the visitors' Peter Robinson. A new star was born as Bastable carried on where he had left off the previous season, leading Cradley to a convincing win. Young Peter Craven was left still trying to score his first point at Dudley Wood!

Only a 4-2 final-heat win by the Bees prevented the Heathens winning at Coventry, but Cradley were beginning to have a solid look about them, with Bastable and Malpass settling into the swing of things from the onset. The rest of the squad were still sorting themselves out, but all of the riders seemed capable of scoring points. Although Yarmouth scored only 27 points at Dudley Wood, Bastable enjoyed one of the shortest reigns as track-record holder as the Bloaters' Bob Baker lowered it to 70.6 seconds in the opening heat of the match.

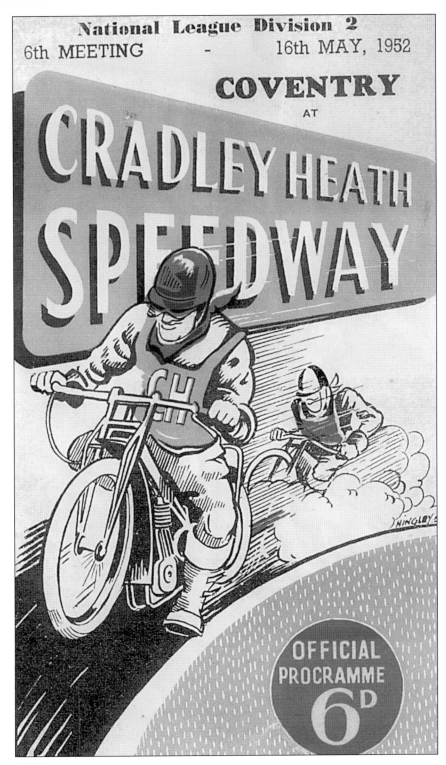

1952 programme cover.

1952 team line-up. From left to right, back row: Wilf Wilstead, Guy Allott, Les Tolley, Harry Bastable, Brian Shepherd. Front row: Derek Braithwaite, Fred Perkins, Phil Malpass, Jim Tolley.

One week later, Harry claimed his first maximum as Cradley crushed White City at Dudley Wood. But as May came around, the Heathens were well beaten at Edinburgh after three punctures and two snapped chains. In addition, Dick Tolley was carried from the track with concussion. Laurie Schofield had so far failed to 'get going' and Don Pettijohn was brought in again, but he failed to make any impact. Brian Shepherd was improving with every match, and Fred Perkins was proving to be a prolific scorer. In fact, the Heathens should have won at Liverpool until Fred fell in heat thirteen and Cradley lost by 4 points.

Stoke and Coventry were well beaten at Dudley Wood and Perkins recorded his first maximum against the Bees. Stoke had no sooner left than they were back, this time in the National Trophy, and the Heathens seemed to be well on their way to the next round with a 26-point advantage under their belts. Stoke, however, had other ideas and on their own track they took full advantage of poor performances by Allott, Shepherd and Jim and Dick Tolley to win the match 71-37 and put Cradley out of the competition. After beating Oxford at Dudley Wood, Cradley headed for Scotland and although they lost both matches, the Heathens were far from disgraced at White City and Motherwell. They exacted swift revenge on Motherwell at Cradley before losing at Yarmouth.

In the Midland Riders' Championship qualifying round at Dudley Wood, Alan Hunt arrived with a point to prove, which he did in his first race win against Bastable. It was the only point that Harry dropped all through the meeting, but Hunt reigned supreme with a 15-point maximum. The Heathens had a disastrous meeting at Poole, losing by 69-15. Only Malpass, who split the Brian Crutcher/Roy Craighead pairing, prevented the Pirates from scoring a maximum possible 70-14 win. Poole were undoubtedly the strongest team in the Second Division, and consequently won the League by 8 clear points.

Cradley 'regrouped' and fought off an Edinburgh challenge to take the League points at Dudley Wood, but one week later, Poole once again got the better of the Heathens, this time at Cradley. The Heathens' reserves had failed to score a single point, and with Bastable and Malpass both suffering a decline in form, a decision was taken to strengthen the squad. Ex-Heathen Geoff Bennett made his return to Dudley Wood after an absence of five years with Birmingham's blessing, as Geoff had broken his leg riding in Ireland in 1951, and it was reckoned that a spell in a lower division would boost his confidence.

He made his debut at Motherwell, scoring 4 points as Cradley lost by 14, and could manage only 5 points in the return the following night at Dudley Wood as Jim Tolley scored his first maximum for the Heathens and led them to a 51-33 win. Fred Perkins' form was a cause for concern. After such a bright start, he had scored only 4 points in the last few matches and Dick Tolley, who looked completely out of touch, was replaced by the ever faithful Wilf Wilstead.

In mid-July, the Heathens produced their best performance of the season when they visited Stoke and took away their 100 per cent home record, winning the match 51-32 with a good all-round performance. Jim and Les Tolley top-scored for Cradley with 11 points as Oxford were well beaten at Dudley Wood and Bastable was unbeaten by an opponent.

The next meeting at Dudley Wood was the World Championship qualifying round, and the largest crowd of the season saw Austrian champion Fritz Dirtl and Scandinavian Basse Hveem. Les Tolley won the meeting from Dirtl, but it was Phil Malpass who made history by becoming the first man ever to break the 70-second time barrier around Dudley Wood when he recorded a new track record of 69.8 seconds – a record that was to stand for many years.

Bastable and Shepherd put up staunch resistance at Ashfield, but did not receive sufficient support to prevent the Heathens from losing by 18 points. Continuing their 'Scottish tour', Cradley enjoyed better fortune at White City as once again, inspired by Bastable and Shepherd, they stormed to a 4-point win. Harry hit top form at the beginning of August. He scored a maximum against Ashfield as the Heathens won at Dudley Wood, followed that with another, as Cradley narrowly lost at Leicester, and scored his third successive maximum as Leicester were beaten at Dudley Wood. On the way to Blackbird Road, Jim Tolley broke down, which may have ultimately cost Cradley the League points at Leicester.

As the month progressed, the Heathens crashed out of the Midland Cup, losing on aggregate to Coventry and were heavily beaten at Yarmouth. A quick team analysis found the majority of points coming from Bastable, Shepherd and Les Tolley. Jim Tolley and Phil Malpass were spasmodically successful, but Perkins had failed to find his earlier form and Geoff Bennett was a shadow of his former self. Guy Allott, after an absence of some weeks, had found points hard to come by. Inconsistency throughout the team became the order of the day, and although league honours seemed to be beyond them, Cradley battled on, beating Yarmouth and Coventry at Dudley Wood and losing at Coventry by 12 points to end the month.

September began brilliantly for the Heathens as they won at home against Stoke and White City, and they continued to take league points at Oxford and Ashfield. Derek Braithwaite had been brought in at reserve and the odd points that he was scoring probably inspired the lesser lights to do better. This resulted in Cradley's fifth consecutive win against a lively Edinburgh side at Dudley Wood. The following evening brought about a reversal of scores at Meadowbank, the Heathens this time being on the wrong end of the 44-40 scoreline, but the bubble burst at Liverpool when the Chads were easy winners with a 56-28 victory.

In the last match of September, Cradley beat Ashfield 45-39 at Dudley Wood and while Bastable, Shepherd, Les and Jim Tolley all scored well, Perkins, Allott, Malpass and Braithwaite scored only 6 points between them. Bastable ended the season on a low note, scoring only 4 points as Cradley crashed to League Champions Poole in the last match of the season at Dudley Wood. He managed only 3 points as the Heathens were crushed in the return at Poole, and his misery was complete as he crashed and was stretchered off the track at Stoke in Cradley's final fixture of 1952. It was not only Cradley's last match of the season – it was their last match for almost seven years!

The Heathens had finished in fourth place in a League of twelve teams which, taking inconsistency into consideration, was quite an achievement. Bastable had been a huge success, averaging 8 points a match with Brian Shepherd just behind him. Jim and Les Tolley had ended the season averaging just over 6 points a match, slightly ahead of Phil Malpass. Perkins, Allott and Bennett had all averaged less than 4 points.

Despite having had a much better season than in 1951, support had been down. The writing was on the wall for Cradley Heathens, and they were destined to be victims in speedway's further decline. As the gates of Dudley Wood Stadium closed at the end of the 1952 season, they would remain so for many years – until 1960, in fact, when speedway returned to the Black Country town of Cradley Heath. For the 1953 season, the Cradley riders joined with Wolverhampton and operated in the Second Division from Monmore Green.

Alan Hunt went on to become Birmingham's top rider and one of England's top performers. He appeared in three World Championship finals, although he failed to do himself justice in any one of them. On 2 February 1957, while riding in South Africa, he crashed and was killed – God bless Alan …

7

RE-BIRTH
1960

Speedway once again found its way in 1960, when the newly formed Provincial League (PL) created a platform upon which the sport could expand. By the end of February, the Speedway Control Board had issued licences to ten tracks in order to form the new League and Cradley was amongst them. It was ruled that no track could have more than three experienced riders (although this proved to be a very flexible ruling) and that no foreigners should be allowed to compete in the new league. Teams would race over twelve heats and the reserve was not programmed to ride. The new promoters were led by Mike Parker and he more than anyone should take credit for the revival in speedway that followed.

Phil Malpass had been running an impressive training school at Dudley Wood during the winter and was named team manager of the new Heathens, who were largely riders from that school. The former Heathen's first signing was Ronnie Rolfe from Southern Area League Ipswich. Ronnie, a former grass-track rider of some note, began riding at Rye House in the winter of 1955/56, and had fought his way into the Rye team by 1957 before moving to Ipswich.

Another grass-track rider of some repute was George Bewley, who had made his speedway debut at California, near Reading, in 1955. Roy Spencer had ridden a handful of meetings in France the previous year, and Vic White, the twenty-eight-year-old from Hackney, along with thirty-one year old Rugby-born Eric Eadon, made up the backbone of a very inexperienced Cradley Heath team. Eric's brother Tony, a former Coventry junior, and Bill Coleman were signed as reserves.

The new Heathens made their debut at Rayleigh on 15 April and lost heavily by 50-20, Eric Eadon topping the Cradley scorechart with 6 points. He and Ronnie Rolf were the only Heathens to win a race. This was hardly surprising as their opponents boasted the likes of Reg Reeves, Pete Lansdale, Eric Hockaday and Alan Smith, all riders of vast experience that made Rayleigh the strongest team in the league by far.

Dudley Wood Stadium re-opened its doors to speedway the following night, when Cradley once more took on the mighty Rayleigh Rockets. Once again it was Eadon and Rolfe who top-scored for the Heathens, this time with 8 points apiece, but although Cradley battled gamely in front of an enthusiastic crowd, they lost the match by 4 points.

The following week, Bristol visited Dudley Wood for a challenge match. The Bulldogs boasted a team almost as strong as Rayleigh, but the Heathens managed to hold them to a draw. Eric Eadon kept up his top-scoring form, this time with 10 points, which entitled him to challenge Bristol's Johnny Hole for the Silver Sash in a match race. Hole made a successful defence, but had to record the fastest time of the night to do so – 75.9 seconds. The track had officially re-opened with the record still being held by Phil Malpass at 69.8 seconds.

Home victories against Bradford, Poole, and Stoke followed with fine performances from Eadon, who was beginning to make a name for himself with two successive maximums. Roy Spencer was turning in some impressive performances, and a young tearaway by the name of Erol Brook was putting himself about a bit in the reserve berth.

In May, Cradley staged a 'Best Pairs' meeting, which only featured contracted Cradley riders, and they seemed to have found another star in the making as Geoff Whitehouse battled his way to 7 points. However, the Eadon brothers stole the show with 19 points, but Geoff was drafted into the team for the next match at Dudley Wood against Edinburgh and obliged with 5 points. Although the Heathens beat the Monarchs by 10 points, they lost Bill Coleman in a heat three crash. A couple of days later, Bill McGregor was at reserve as Cradley won by 2 points at Liverpool, but in doing so they lost the ever-improving Vic White in a final-heat crash.

Harry Bastable had been the top Cradley rider when the stadium had closed in 1952, but from the minute he moved on, his promising career went into decline. At Wolverhampton, Birmingham and especially Leicester, he was a shadow of his former

1960 team line-up. From left to right: Tony Eadon, Eric Eadon, George Bewley, Ronnie Rolf (on machine), Phil Malpass, Harry Bastable, Ray Spencer, Vic White. (Speedway Star)

CRADLEY

HEATH

SPEEDWAY

Provincial League Championship

CRADLEY HEATH

v

EDINBURGH

Official Programme - 6d.

1960 programme cover.

Eric Eadon. (Speedway Star)

Harry Bastable. (Speedway Star)

Ronnie Rolf. (Speedway Star)

Roy Spencer. (Speedway Star)

self, probably because his heart was at Dudley Wood. Harry had made it known that he was interested in joining the new Heathens and had even built up one of his old bikes and presented it to them for a track spare. In June, his wish was finally granted and Leicester allowed him to return to his beloved Cradley Heath for a £50 transfer fee.

It was the best money Cradley had ever spent. Harry made his debut at Dudley Wood on 6 June in a challenge match against Aldershot. He rolled back the years to go through the card unbeaten, and to lead Cradley (who were without Bewley, White, Coleman and Whitehouse) to a 7-point victory. The Heathens' League campaign continued halfway through the month with away wins at Bradford and Liverpool as well as a win at Dudley Wood against Liverpool. Cradley had taken that first step away from persevering with a completely inexperienced team, and Bastable had fused them into a team to be feared at home or away.

In just a few weeks, Harry had established himself as one of the top stars in the Provincial League, and his scores were rarely other than double figures. The new League had saved many riders such as Bastable from certain extinction and now, reborn, they were once again stars in their own right. The likes of Pete Lansdale, Ray Harris, Wal Morton and Reg Reeves, to name but a few, had their racing careers extended by many years, thanks to the Provincial League.

Cradley moved into July with Bastable consistently brilliant both home and away, and Rolfe, Spencer and Eadon all scoring well, but as the month progressed, the form of the latter three took a turn for the worse, and heavy defeats at Eastbourne and Wigan followed. An embarrassing 29-42 defeat at Dudley Wood by the mighty Poole saw Bastable take on the Pirates virtually on his own, and he claimed the new Provincial track record of 72.3 seconds. While Harry grew in stature, there was a steady downward trend in the form of Eric Eadon, and defeats at St Austell, Sheffield and Edinburgh were to follow.

Bastable's virtual one-man crusade was unable to stop defeats at Yarmouth and Stoke and another defeat at Dudley Wood against Sheffield. Cradley's purple patch had indeed come to an abrupt halt. However, Harry once again gave the fans something to cheer about in the Dudley Wood qualifying round of the Provincial League Riders' Championship. Although he finished second to the wily Trevor Redmond, the Cradley favourite beat Jack Kitchen for the Silver Sash, lowering the track record to 71.6 seconds in the process.

With Bewley injured again, Geoff Whitehouse announcing his retirement, and Roy Spencer's loss of form, Cradley drafted in Norwich junior Clive Featherby, who immediately made an impression by top-scoring with 9 points at Stoke. He followed this by failing to score at Dudley Wood against a winning Bristol team in a match which saw Trevor Redmond relieve Bastable of the Silver Sash. In the Heathens' last home League match, a win against Sheffield, Featherby scored 11 points. He was an enigma, and remained so for the rest of his long career.

The final fixture at Dudley Wood in 1960 was a feather in their cap, if ever there was one. Cradley Heath had been chosen to host the Provincial League Riders' Championship. The irony of it was that although Harry Bastable had qualified, he was unable to take his place, due to him pre-booking a holiday abroad (which Mrs Bastable was determined to take). The curtain came down on Cradley's first season back in speedway with Trevor Redmond being crowned Provincial League Riders' Champion, with Poole's Ken Middleditch the runner-up and Rayleigh's Eric Hockaday in third place in a great meeting with some first-class racing.

Rayleigh, as expected, won the League, losing only two matches. Poole were second and Bristol third, with Cradley finishing a creditable sixth, and the incredible Harry Bastable topped the Heathens' averages with 11.66 points a match. Eric Eadon followed with 7.11 and Ronnie Rolfe averaged 5.55. In its first year, the Provincial League had been a huge success, and while its counterpart the National League was struggling, despite its Fundins, Briggs, Cravens, and Moores, the future seemed assured for the likes of Cradley Heath for many years to come. The fans had got back their taste for speedway back and couldn't wait for the gates to re-open in April 1961.

8

THE WHITE GHOST OF
DUDLEY WOOD
1961

The year 1961 saw ex-Heathen Roy Moreton take over as team manager as Phil Malpass was unable to travel to away meetings due to his commitments as a journalist. Promoter Morris Jephcott made one of his shrewder moves when he signed Ivor Brown from Yarmouth, but with respect to Mr Jephcott, he could not possibly have known what an impact Brown would have on the Provincial League.

Ivor began speedway in 1952, riding in second-half events at Long Eaton. Upon their closure, he had a short spell at Birmingham before moving to Leicester in 1953 where he remained, confined to the second halves, until 1958. He was then loaned to Junior League Yarmouth, where he began to make progress. Yarmouth joined the Provincial League in its initial year, and skipper Ivor really began to come into his own, averaging almost 10 points a match and reaching the Provincial Riders' final at Cradley. Yarmouth closed down at the end of the 1960 season, and the Cradley management pulled off a major coup by signing the Leicestershire grocer.

Another new face at Dudley Wood was twenty-one-year-old John Hart, son of former Brummie rider Phil 'Tiger' Hart. Racing was in John's blood, and he was racing stock cars around Hednesford raceway before his eighteenth birthday. In 1969, he had his first taste of speedway in the second half at Stoke before being snapped up by the Heathens.

Hart and Brown were joined by Harry Bastable, Vic White, Ronnie Rolfe and the Eadon brothers for Cradley's opening match at Stoke on the last day of March. The Potters' Ken Adams won the first race at Sun Street, knocking 2.4 seconds off the track record and beating Bastable in the process, but Harry had his revenge in heat five when he beat Adams and equalled the new record. Ivor Brown made his debut with an immaculate 15-point maximum, but, apart from Bastable and Brown, the rest of the team were disappointing and Stoke won this new thirteen-heat formula match by 44-34.

Cradley made their home debut next night with a re-match against the Potters, and introduced their new signing from New Cross, thirty-three-year-old Derek Timms. Birmingham-born Derek began speedway in 1951 with Wolverhampton, mixing speedway with grass-track and scrambling before moving to Aldershot and then on to New Cross. Derek will always be remembered for his affable manner and his rather

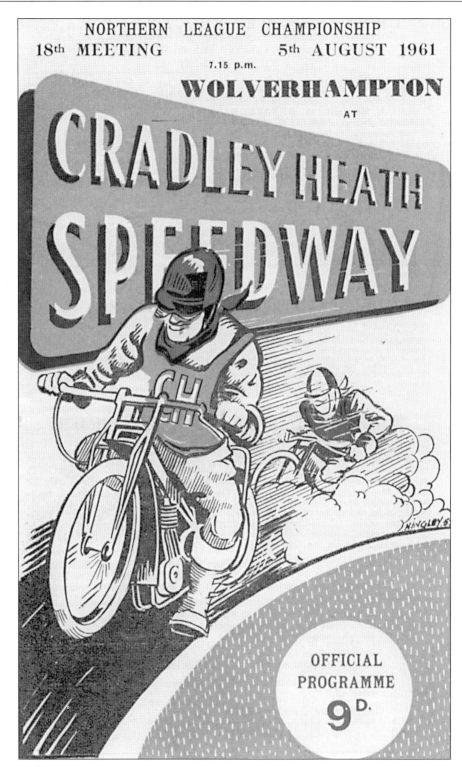

1961 programme cover.

large paunch, which he tended to rest on the frame of his machine as he was hurtling around the track. He was a great tryer and it was hoped that he would fill the gap created by the dissatisfied Clive Featherby. Featherby, who could be a difficult man, had moved on to Sheffield, where he was to become one of the most prolific scorers in the League.

Derek scored 4 points in his home debut and Bastable dropped only 1 point. Brown was again unbeaten and the Heathens won 42-36. It was to be Eric Eadon's last appearance for Cradley, for he could muster only 1 point, as he had done at Stoke the previous night, and he was transferred to newcomers Wolverhampton.

The Provincial League looked a little different from the previous year, having lost Bristol, Yarmouth, Bradford and Liverpool, and having gained Wolverhampton, Plymouth, Exeter, Middlesbrough and Newcastle. The legendary Cradley/Wolves matches were about to begin and bring to the fans some of the most exciting matches ever to be seen in speedway.

Faithful George Bewley was brought in to replace Eadon, but with Hart, Tony Eadon and Vic White struggling, the Heathens lost their next two away matches and won their next two home matches by only 2 points. Moreton, in a desperate attempt to strengthen the bottom end of the team, brought back Roy Spencer, but he failed to respond. However, he then cast his eyes to the second half where local youngster Alan Totney was making waves, beating the likes of John Hart and Derek Timms, and towards the end of April, Alan made his debut for Cradley at Middlesbrough, scoring 2 points.

Totney was always a great favourite with fans because besides his never-say-die attitude, he was a local lad who lived just a stone's throw from the stadium. Alan continued to score steadily over the next few weeks and became a team regular.

At the end of the month, Rayleigh came calling and although the champions were not the force they had been the previous year, they had retained the services of the brilliant Reg Reeves. Cradley won the match 43-35, but Reeves equalled the track record and went through the card unbeaten – no mean feat in those days when Bastable and Brown were continually battling to be 'King of Dudley Wood'. This was Ronnie Rolfe's last match in the green and white before he was transferred to Sheffield.

The Heathens' next match was at Dudley Wood and as they thrashed Middlesbrough, Derek Timms came good and scored his first Cradley maximum. The following Friday saw Cradley make their debut at Monmore Green in a League encounter that was to be the first of many local derbies. Wolverhampton had built their team around the legendary Graham Warren. True, the several-times world finalist had seen better days, but this was the Provincial League where the ex-stars were now the new stars, and Warren was undoubtedly in this category. His battles with Ivor Brown were to become part of Cradley folklore and both being showmen, their mutual dislike for each other was hyped up to fever pitch by both teams' promoters alike. Brown immediately settled down on the tricky Monmore circuit and scored the first of many maximums that he was to record at Wolverhampton, much to the frustration of the Wolves supporters. He led the Heathens to a 45-33 victory, and the next night at Cradley the Heathens won again by the same score, but this time it was Warren who was unbeaten.

Meanwhile, Alan Totney had broken a finger and was sidelined and junior Mike Wilmore took his place. However, Mike was finding the pace a little too hot and with Cradley at the top of the League, and Brown in fifth place in the League Riders' averages, the management was desperate to keep up the impetus. As a result, Harry Bastable talked his old mate Ivor Davies out of retirement.

Ivor 'Digger' Davies was a thirty-year-old farmer-cum-greengrocer who had been out of speedway for seven years, but Harry was sure that he was the man to help the Heathens to their first League title. Digger made his first appearance in Cradley colours at Edinburgh, where he blew up his engine in the first race and failed to score. In the same fateful match, George Bewley took a tumble that put him out of the team for the rest of the season.

In the return match at Dudley Wood, a maximum by Brown entitled him to challenge veteran Dick Campbell for the Silver Sash. Ivor became the new holder and he retained the Match Race Championship, defending it against the likes of Tommy Roper, Clive Featherby, Don Wilkinson and Rick France, before relinquishing it at Stoke to veteran Ray Harris.

The end of May saw Brown and Bastable clash for the first time, at Dudley Wood in the qualifying round of the World Championship. It was a storybook finish, as they both tied on 13 points, 1 point better than the National League's Peter Vandenberg. Harry got the better of Ivor in the run-off, as he did in the qualifying round of the Provincial Riders' Championship. On that occasion, Bastable scored a 15-point maximum to head Ivor by just a point.

Over the next couple of weeks, Davies began to settle down and score steadily, as did Tony Eadon, and with Bastable and Brown almost always scoring double figures, Cradley picked up a couple of away wins at Middlesbrough and Newcastle. But Vic White had been point-less for two matches, and his form was causing concern – so much so that, as soon as Totney declared himself fit, he was reinstated.

17 June saw the first ever leg of the now legendary Dudley/Wolves Trophy at Dudley Wood. A thrilling match saw Brown, Bastable and Warren all drop points, and Wolves returned to Monmore 3 points adrift. The return leg saw some stirring stuff by Warren and Vic Ridgeon for the Wolves and Brown, Bastable and Timms for Cradley, but Wolves won on aggregate 97-94 and a speedway institution was born.

The following night, the Heathens went to Stoke and knocked the Potters out of the Knockout Cup. However, at Dudley Wood a week later, in a meaningless challenge match against Rayleigh, Totney made his return. After winning his first ever race for Cradley, he crashed, broke two ribs and a collarbone, and was out again!

It was around this time that Ivor Brown became the 'White Ghost of Dudley Wood'. Ivor, probably thinking that he was a little bit different from his peers, decided to look a little different also and began to wear a white jersey over the top of his leathers with his Cradley bib over that. In the days of dull black leathers, this was quite an innovation and with loads of dirt on the tracks in those days, quite a brave one – perhaps it gave him even more incentive to be at the front, for it was not Ivor's way to be shabby. In fact, 'immaculate' is a word that described Ivor in every way. It conveyed his appearance, his machinery, his riding and even his transport!

1961 team line-up. From left to right: Mike Wilmore, John Hart, Tony Eadon, George Bewley, Ivor Brown, Harry Bastable, Derek Timms. (Speedway Star)

In those days, riders would turn up in all manner of vehicles – old vans, Ford Consuls with the back seats ripped out, old bangers towing riffy trailers and so on. Alan Totney had even been known to push his bike to the stadium! But Mr Brown always arrived in his shimmering Jaguar, towing a spotless trailer. It said everything about the man. A quiet bachelor, he lived in the quiet village of Wymeswold, where he quietly ran his village shop, enjoyed a quiet game of cricket and got up at the crack of dawn every morning to take on his role of village postman. But on a couple of nights a week, Jekyll turned into Hyde as the white jersey was donned and he wreaked havoc upon all of his opponents.

His distinctive riding style won him admirers and enemies alike. He was a 'white line specialist' and if he missed the gate, he would line up behind the leader and push and cajole him until he would either move over or get his foot run over! He quickly became 'the man they love to hate' – the Provincial League's Ove Fundin, if you like – and as his reputation preceded him, the away track supporters practised booing the week before he was due to ride. Brownie revelled in the attention, and it merely inspired him to greater achievements. He was hated at away tracks, but at Dudley Wood, he was worshipped.

Cradley continued their League campaign, bringing junior Bruce Cooley in at reserve. Bruce failed to score in his first two matches and never even looked like gaining any points, so Cradley entered the transfer market. Stan Stevens was a twenty-six-year-old jobbing printer from London, who rode at Rye House in 1959 and joined Rayleigh for their Championship season in 1960. He was considered to be one of the

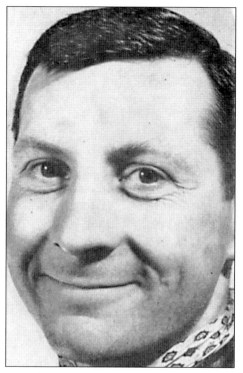

Vic White. (Speedway Star) *Derek Timms.* (Speedway Star)

brightest prospects in the game and was tipped for stardom. Cradley snapped him up in mid-July for the princely sum of £200, and Stan appeared for the Heathens for the first time at Dudley Wood against opponents Sheffield.

He got off to an unbelievable start, scoring a maximum on his debut, but so did Brown, Bastable and Digger Davies, and the result was one of the Heathens' biggest ever wins, 60-18. Stevens was unbeaten again his next match, a challenge against Yarmouth Select. Everything in the garden looked rosy, with Cradley boasting the best two signings in the League, but the Heathens were forced to entertain Poole in a Knockout Cup match without the 'cup-tied' Stevens.

Even so, with White, Timms, Hart and Tony Eadon chipping in points, Cradley were a match for any team at Dudley Wood. They duly dispatched Poole, who at that time were probably the best Provincial League outfit in the country, but they did so at a price. Digger Davies, who was showing his best form since his return, had dropped only 1 point when he crashed in heat nine and was taken to hospital with facial injuries. But Cradley were through to the final.

Without Davies, Cradley lost heavily at Exeter and Poole. Hart, Timms and White scored only 2 points between the three of them in both matches. It was the same story at Plymouth, and the rot continued at Dudley Wood, as visitors Poole clinched the match by 2 points. Brown was still piling up the points, but Bastable was going through a lean spell by his own high standards. After a brilliant start, Stevens had become 'Mr

Inconsistency', and Timms, Hart and White were right out of it. Cradley began to plummet in the League.

Mid-August saw the return of Davies at the expense of Johnny Hart, and with him came the return of the Heathens' form. Newcastle were thrashed 59-19 at Dudley Wood, and Bastable was back to his best when leading Cradley to wins at Bradford and Newcastle.

Next on the agenda was the Knockout Cup final against Edinburgh in the last Heathens home match of the season. Not many teams had won at Edinburgh, and Cradley knew that a good lead in the first leg at Dudley Wood was imperative if they were to lift the cup. All of the Heathens rode like heroes and the Monarchs were slaughtered 68-28. In the second leg at Meadowbank, the Heathens were indeed beaten, but came out winners on aggregate, 102-57. Bastable top-scored with only 7 points, but everyone chipped in with points and Cradley won their first major trophy.

In the wind-up to the season, Brown inevitably left his mark. He scored an incredible 17 points for the Provincial League Select side against a National League Select side at Monmore Green, and also won the Battle of Britain Trophy at Stoke. In the Provincial League Riders' Championship at Harringay, won by the mercurial Reg Reeves, Ivor could only manage fourth place with 11 points, with Stan Stevens also scoring 11 and Harry Bastable 10.

The Heathens finished the season in fourth place (behind Poole, Plymouth and Stoke) and lost the Northern League by only 2 points. Brown was top scorer in the League with 461 points and a $11\frac{1}{2}$-point average, Ken Adams followed with 374 points and good old Harry Bastable was third with 367 points. It had been a good year for Cradley. The team was almost unrecognisable from the 1960 squad, and the changes made had been reflected in the success that they had achieved. Provincial League fans just couldn't get enough. On Boxing Day, Cradley competed in a four-team tournament at Stoke. They finished in second place, and Ivor Brown scored the almost inevitable maximum.

9

NOTHING GOING ON
1962

Cradley's season began as strangely as it had ended the year before. After finishing on the previous Boxing Day, the Dudley Wood Stadium gates opened the following February. The occasion was the BBC *Grandstand* Best Pairs Trophy. The Trophy, which featured some of the best riders in the Provincial League, was run over two consecutive Saturday afternoons at Cradley and live coverage was broadcast on the BBC's *Grandstand* programme. It was certainly a feather in Cradley's cap, and was also an indication as to how much interest had been revived in speedway.

In the first meeting, Cradley pairs took the first three places – Bastable and Hart, followed by Davies and Timms and then Brown and Tony Eadon. The following Saturday afternoon, Brown and Eadon won the event from Stoke's Ray Harris and Peter Jarman. It has to be said that the meetings were rather poor affairs, with hardly any racing, and the general opinion was that they had done the sport no favours whatsoever media-wise. The gates closed for a while and re-opened on 7 April with an unchanged Heathens side. Bewley had recovered from his injuries and lined up alongside Stevens, Timms, Brown, Bastable, Hart and Davies. Brown started off slowly and rode three matches before he finally hit double figures in Cradley's second home meeting, when he scored a maximum and the Heathens won the Iron and Steel Trophy by beating Sheffield.

The serious stuff began with a Midland League match at Stoke, which the home side narrowly won, but the Potters' Ken Adams was forced to surrender the Silver Sash to Ivor Brown. Ivor successfully defended it against young Johnny Edwards the following night at Dudley Wood when Cradley easily beat Stoke in the reverse fixture. Brown, Bastable and Stevens were all scoring well, but the other four Heathens were finding life difficult in the increasingly competitive League.

Cradley continued their Midland League campaign with a visit to Wolverhampton at the end of April, where they lost by only 2 points. Brown won only one race and even came third in the last heat behind Graham Warren and the sensational youngster Terry Betts, as the Monmore terraces went ballistic. The Wolves fans held their breath as Warren lined up to make his Silver Sash challenge. He was unbeaten so far and Brownie was having an 'off night' – surely Graham would bring the Sash to Monmore Green. Typically, Ivor had saved his best until last and, much to the fury and frustration of the Wolverhampton fans, he rode like a demon to retain the Silver Sash.

In the corresponding fixture the following night at Dudley Wood, Brown bounced back to form, scoring a maximum, and he once again defeated Warren in the Match

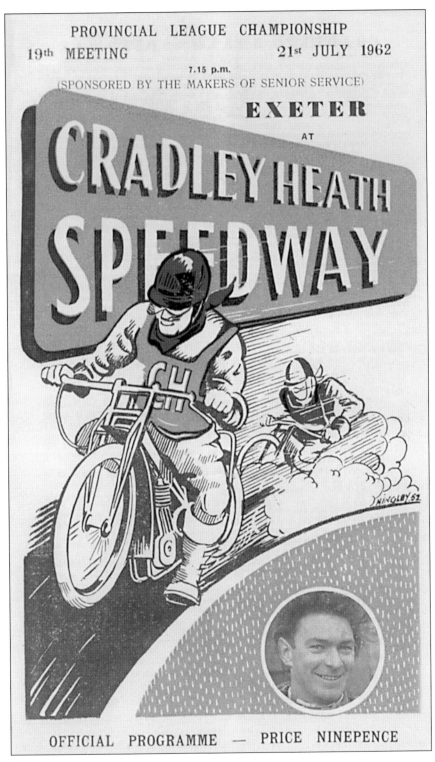

1962 programme cover.

1962 team line-up. From left to right: Derek Timms (kneeling), George Bewley, Ivor Brown, Ivor 'Digger' Davies (on machine), Harry Bastable, Alan Totney, John Hart, Stan Stevens (kneeling). (Speedway Star)

Race Championship. The Heathens made no mistakes either and vanquished the Wolves 56-22. Cradley completed their Midland League fixtures against the newly conscripted Leicester Hunters. They lost at Blackbird Road and won at Dudley Wood, Ivor defending the Sash successfully against Slant Payling on both occasions. The Heathens' away performances in the Midland League had let them down, and they had to settle for second place behind Wolverhampton in the competition.

The second week in May saw the start of the League competition. Brown was riding at his brilliant best, Bastable was riding well, Davies was settling down and John Hart was beginning to put some good scores together. With Stevens and Timms riding inconsistently, the Cradley management began to look at the reserve berth.

George Bewley was struggling, so before each match he was required to ride in a run-off with Alan Totney and Tony Eadon for the reserve spot. Totney was the man who lined up with the Heathens to take on Champions Poole in Cradley's first League match at Dudley Wood. The twenty-seven-year-old had shown great pace in 1961, and Cradley were looking for him to regain his form.

Cradley battled gamely to beat the Pirates by 2 points, all the Heathens scoring solidly, but the star of the night was the Poole veteran Tony Lewis. On the night he was in a different class to everyone else and stormed through the card completely untroubled, easily beating Brown in the Silver Sash Match Race.

The Heathens made their way through May winning their home matches and losing their away ones. Brown was still scoring double figures and occasionally Bastable, or even Hart, would join him. In fact, every Heathen was capable of scoring well, but they were failing to do it on the same night. When it did happen, such as at Neath at the beginning of June, they won. The rest of the month saw them win four matches – all at Dudley Wood – and lo and behold, Cradley found themselves at the top of the Provincial League. However, skipper Bastable injured his wrist and was out for three weeks, and when George Bewley was drafted back into the side, Tony Eadon, seeing his chance had gone once again, moved on to Leicester.

After getting knocked out of the Knockout Cup at Middlesbrough, Cradley moved on to Poole and had a disastrous match against the very strong Pirates, losing the match 54-23. Brown unsuccessfully challenged Lewis for the Silver Sash, but, more importantly, acting skipper Digger Davies joined the injured list with a fractured leg that ended his season. The Heathens called in junior Joe Westwood for a visit to Edinburgh, and an inevitable defeat was the result.

Bastable made a premature return for the Dudley/Wolves Trophy, scoring only 2 points at Monmore but managing 10 points at Dudley Wood. His efforts were not enough to prevent Wolves from retaining the trophy, however, with a 7-point aggregate win. Cradley had found a replacement for Davies in National League Coventry's Nick Nicholls. Nick had been finding the pace a little too hot in the NL and had been given the Bees' blessing to ride in the Provincial League. He made his debut in the Dudley Wood leg of the Dudley/Wolves Trophy and scored a creditable 7 points.

Three consecutive defeats followed – Cradley were even unable to beat Trevor Redmond's inexperienced Neath at Dudley Wood – and the Heathens went tumbling down the League table. Brown, unaffected by his team-mates' inconsistency, soldiered

John Hart. (Speedway Star)   *Stan Stevens.* (Speedway Post)

Ivor 'Digger' Davies.
(Speedway Star)

on. In fact he hit top form and took the Silver Sash from ex-Heathen Eric Boothroyd at Middlesbrough, but the White Ghost was receiving little support as Bastable struggled away from home. Stan Stevens began to look like he would never achieve what he had so richly promised. Nicholls had settled into middle scoring, and Hart and Timms occasionally joined him, but on the whole, the Heathens at this time were a pretty uninspired bunch.

Ivor defended the Sash against Exeter's veteran Pete Lansdale at Dudley Wood, before losing it at Plymouth to the evergreen Jimmy Squibb. Cradley continued winning at home and losing away into August, until they faced a weakened Poole team at Dudley Wood. Despite a 15-point Brown maximum, the Heathens lost by 2 points – but there was unrest in the camp. Johnny Hart walked out after being replaced in heat six, and Stan Stevens was reprimanded for 'showing no effort whatsoever' – always a good morale booster!

In their next match at Cradley (without Hart), the Heathens crushed Newcastle thanks to a fine maximum from Nick Nicholls, but this was not to be Cradley's year. A couple of nights later, Nicholls crashed at Exeter, sustained severe concussion and subsequently announced his retirement from speedway.

At the beginning of September, Hart returned to Dudley Wood and, as if to prove a point, scored a brilliant maximum against Wolves to lead the Heathens to a comfortable win. Not so comfortable, however, was Stan Stevens. A lacklustre performance netted him only 2 points and he was dropped from the team.

Stan's replacement for the next match at home against Stoke was John Belcher. John was an ex-Oxford junior who had been given some second-half races at Dudley Wood and with respect to the youngster, it must have been a smack in the face for Stan to be replaced by a novice. Belcher made the perfect debut, following Derek Timms home for a 5-1 in his first race; however, those 2 points were the only ones that he scored in the match. It was not Cradley's night and after losing Johnny Hart in a first-heat crash, the Heathens conceded the match by 6 points.

Cradley's final meeting of the season at Dudley Wood was a challenge match between the Heathens Past and the Heathens Present. The 'Past' featured Graham Warren, Vic White, Tony Eadon, Guy Allott and Clive Featherby, and they won the rather low-key affair by 2 points. Cradley lost their last two away meetings at Wolverhampton and Bradford, finishing in a disappointing eighth place in a League of thirteen. Poole retained the League Championship.

Towards the end of September at Stoke, Ivor Brown once again starred for the 'Provincials' against the 'Nationals', scoring 15 points and beating the mighty Nigel Boocock in the process. Brownie had a disastrous Provincial League Riders' final, scoring only 7 points, and he even fell to second place in the League Scorers behind Eric Boothroyd. He did, however, win the Champion of Champions Trophy at Monmore and finished top of the Cradley averages with 10.8 points. Harry Bastable followed him with 7.5, and John Hart, who had finished runner-up in the Provincial League Midland Riders' Championship, averaged 6.0 points.

It had been a poor season for the Heathens: one that had promised so much and had yielded so little. Harry Bastable suffered injuries and rode when he really should not have done, as his large drop in average suggests. Harry missed his first ever matches for Cradley in 1962. Nick Nicholls, after flourishing briefly, was out, as was Ivor Davies, and Stan Stevens had become an enigma. The only pleasing point was the progress of Johnny Hart, but the fiery Heathen ended the season by putting in a transfer request.

The Provincial League had exceeded everyone's expectations with its competitiveness and its quality of riders and racing. In a mere couple of seasons, it had achieved what it had set out to do by forming a league that had the unique combination of youth and experience. The older riders, of which there were many, would surely see out the remainder of their careers in the new league, whilst passing on their expertise and experience to their up-and-coming counterparts, who would indeed use the league as a training ground to propel them to the very top of the sport. Cradley Heathens had learned a lesson – there were no easy pickings in the Provincial League.

10
CUP KILLERS
1963

Stan Stevens had been transferred to New Cross, Nick Nicholls and George Bewley had retired, and Digger Davies was still suffering from the injuries that he had sustained the previous season, so Cradley began the 1963 season right in the mire. They had applied for, and been given, permission to sign another heat-leader. They approached, amongst others, National League dropout Bob Duckworth and Wimbledon's Jim Tebby, but in the event Tebby stayed put and Duckworth joined Newcastle.

Promoter Jephcott got so frustrated that he threatened not to re-open, but fortunately he saw sense and went ahead. After all, he still had 'The Firm' – Bastable and Brown. Timms and Totney were still on board and Johnny Hart had come to his senses and also signed on. Ivor Davies signed too, but he fell in practice and was ordered away by his doctor. So Cradley began their 1963 campaign recognised by the 'powers that be' as being under-strength and continued searching for that elusive missing heat-leader.

The Heathens began the season with away and home challenge matches against arch-enemy Wolverhampton. Good old George Bewley was asked to temporarily postpone his retirement and he took his place alongside John Belcher in the reserve berths. Cradley lost both matches, emphasising their plight, but Brown was unbeaten and broke the Monmore Green track record in his first race of the season. He went through the card unbeaten as Cradley lost at Sheffield and continued his unblemished run as the Heathens surprisingly won at Stoke in the Midland League, Ivor picking up another track record.

In the return at Dudley Wood, he again proved that he was master of the rest. Five matches into the season, and the brilliant Brown had still not dropped a single point! The Heathens beat Stoke in the Cradley leg and the main reason for this, Brownie excluded, was the blinding form of Hart and Totney, who both scored maximums.

Brown had a nightmare match against Sheffield in the Iron and Steel Trophy match at Dudley Wood and dropped his first points of the season, but Hart carried on and scored his second consecutive maximum. It was not enough to save the Heathens, however, and they lost the match and also the Trophy. George Bewley had stepped down to give young Joe Westwood a crack at reserve but Joe struggled, and an alarming lack of form by Harry Bastable was making the Heathens look a

1963 programme cover.

1963 team line-up. From left to right, back row: John Belcher, Alan Totney, John Edwards. Front row: Harry Bastable, Ivor Brown, John Hart. (Speedway Star)

decidedly fragile outfit. However, Hart was going like a steam train and Totney was riding out of his skin and this covered Harry's shortfall to some extent.

Totney notched up another maximum at Dudley Wood against Long Eaton in a Midland League match and added a bit of unscheduled excitement whilst trying to avoid Archers' Charlie Monk in heat six when he scattered officials and rakers standing near the starting gate!

A visit to Wolverhampton saw the Heathens take a thrashing at the hands of a vastly improved Wolves team. The Monmore Green outfit had added Maurie Mattingly and Les Jenkins to their ranks, and were formidable opposition. Only Brown scored double figures and he was beaten by Ernie Baker.

Cradley won the return the following night at Dudley Wood and fielded their new signing – Dave Hankins. Dave was a former National League rider with Leicester, but had been out of the saddle for eighteen months through injury. He made a pointless debut as the Heathens scraped home by 4 points. In fact, Dave made only one more appearance before calling it a day.

Around this time, a fellow by the name of Lyn Brown came on the scene at Dudley Wood. Lyn hailed from the West Indies, and this rather portly gentleman had aspirations of being a speedway rider. His debut second-half appearance saw him lapped by all of the other riders in the race, so further outings saw him start 150 yards ahead of the likes of Joe Westwood, Ken Sambidge, Freddie Priest and Frank Holmes, but still he failed to score.

To conclude April, Cradley visited Long Eaton, where a win would assure them of the Midland League Championship. In his first ride on the track, Brown broke the track record (making four that he held) and was unbeaten in the match. Good support by Timms, Totney and Hart put the season's first silverware in the Cradley cabinet.

Ivor began May by winning the Monmore Green Trophy from Graham Warren with a 15-point maximum. Pete Jarman was in third place and was closely followed by Ivan Mauger, the sensational Kiwi who was making his debut in the Provincial League with Newcastle. Ivor was really flying by this time, and the next two home matches saw him score maximums against Poole and St Austell. A subsequent trip to Exeter proved costly for the Heathens, because not only did they lose the match, they also lost Alan Totney, who fell and was injured.

For their next match, at Dudley Wood against Middlesbrough, the depleted Heathens recalled George Bewley, and with Belcher and Westwood already in the side, the Cradley bottom end looked suspect to say the least. Joe understandably struggled, but Johnny Belcher was an out-and-out trier, who managed to score points in every match – 2 here, 3 there, but they all counted, and with Harry Bastable now usually in the lower end of the scoring, John's contributions were more than gratefully received. However, Hart, Brown and Timms were not enough to contain the Bears and Middlesbrough won the match by 6 points, but Hart gave the fans something to cheer when he relieved young Eric Boocock of the Silver Sash.

Manager Roy Moreton had never given up his quest to find the missing rider and, towards the end of May, his labours were rewarded. Stoke had decided to place Johnny Edwards on the transfer list. John had ridden for the Potters in 1961 and 1962 but an accident on the way to Middlesbrough which wrote off most of his equipment had put him out of speedway for the best part of 1962, and John had returned to his old job as an engineering draughtsman. He purchased new equipment in the winter and lined up with Stoke at the start of the season, but after only one match he found himself surplus to requirements. He was snapped up by Cradley and began with a steady 5 points at Dudley Wood, when the Heathens beat Hackney (Hart lost the Sash to Norman Hunter). He followed that with 6 points when Cradley lost at Sheffield, but as Brown and Hart scored at the top end, John was strengthening the middle, and Joe Westwood returned to second-half racing.

The start of June saw Totney return to score 10 points in a full-strength Heathen team that flattened visiting Rayleigh. Meanwhile Brown was on a roll, churning out maximums, breaking the Sheffield track record and generally establishing himself as the top man in the Provincial League – bar none. The previous week had seen him win the Archers Trophy from Norman Hunter and Hart at Long Eaton. Ivor had dropped only 1 point in his World Championship qualifying rounds but, as he often seemed to do so on the big occasions, he failed to get through the Provincial Riders' final of the World Championship at Edinburgh.

Mid-month saw the Heathens at Mike Parker's Newcastle and many waited to see how Brown would fare against the rapidly improving Ivan Mauger. They met twice in the match and Mauger won both encounters, issuing a warning to Ivor of his intentions to be top man in the League. They were the only 2 points dropped by the Heathen, but poor support meant a 45-33 defeat. Brown seemed unperturbed, however, and ended the month with two maximums and began July with another two.

Cradley began July by winning the Dudley/Wolves Trophy for the first time, and staged the first ever Alan Hunt Memorial Trophy meeting. It seemed only justice that the first winner was Ivor Brown, who won from Jimmy Squibb and Eric Boocock.

Cradley progressed through the month, mainly winning at home and losing away. All the riders, Brown and Hart apart, had good and bad matches alike and then came the match against New Cross at Dudley Wood on 20 July. Brown came out in the opening heat and shaved more than two seconds off the track record! The crowd gasped as a time of 68.2 seconds was announced. There was a pause as the timekeeper announced that he had made a mistake; confusion was the order of the day, as the time was reinstated and Brown was recognised as the fastest man ever to have ridden four laps of the Dudley Wood circuit. That record stood for many years.

Meanwhile, Ivor Davies had made a comeback against all the odds and quickly moved into middle-order scoring. Cradley were now as strong as they were going to get, but there was still no one getting up there to take the load with Brown and Hart. The Heathens took a hammering at Stoke and Ivor had to concede defeat twice to their new up-and-coming star – a man who would feature significantly in Cradley's history – Colin Pratt.

Early August saw the Heathens again face Stoke, this time at Dudley Wood, in their first Knockout Cup match of the season. Bastable came good at the right time and Brown exacted his revenge on Pratt as Cradley moved into the semi-final with a 55-41 win. Once again the Heathens had drawn a home tie in the competition and Sheffield were swept away 61-35 to send Cradley into the Knockout Cup final. Brown again won the Silver Sash after the match, courtesy of Clive Featherby.

The next few matches reflected the Heathens' new-found confidence as they lost by only a single point at Monmore Green, and mercilessly thrashed Wolves, Stoke and Newcastle at Cradley. Brown defended the Sash against Cyril Francis, Dave Hemus and Colin Pratt before conceding it to Mauger when the Kiwi was unbeaten in Newcastle's visit to Dudley Wood. The 53-25 win against Newcastle was an interesting result because the Diamonds were to be Cradley's opponents in the Knockout Cup final. Also, it had been Ivan Mauger's first visit to Dudley Wood. He had remained unbeaten and had relieved Brown of the Sash. The Provincial crown was beginning to rest uneasily on Brown's head.

Meanwhile, back in the second halves, Lyn Brown was now starting half a lap in front of the others in the Opportunity Stakes and was still trailing in last! Mauger, almost inevitably won the Provincial League Riders' Championship at Belle Vue, while Brown finished ninth in an event in which he never gave a good account of himself.

If Cradley had thought themselves unfortunate at the start of the season, then

Ivor Brown – the 'White Ghost of Dudley Wood'. (Speedway Post)

what was in store for them would certainly make up for that. They were dealt a sickening blow as Hart was pronounced unfit for the first leg of the Knockout Cup final at Newcastle as he was laid up with 'flu. For the Diamonds, the same fate had befallen the mighty Mauger, but that was not the extent of their problems. They

Ivor Brown (left) in action. (Speedway Star)

were also missing their second star man, Brian Craven, and Bob Duckworth too.

On the last day of September, the Heathens lost the first leg at Borough Park but by only 5 points, with skipper Bastable typically riding his heart out for 12 vital points. Cradley had gone to Newcastle with only six men and had only one representative in four races; they lost Davies once more with a broken shoulder, but held on grimly. Top-scoring Ivor Brown claimed the Silver Sash by default, and the Heathens must have fancied their chances in the second leg at Dudley Wood on 12 October.

Prior to that, Cradley were beaten by 10 points at Long Eaton, and Brown lost the Sash to another up-and-coming star, Charlie Monk.

In the second leg of the Knockout Cup final at Cradley, there were to be no mistakes. The Diamonds were strengthened by Duckworth's return but were still without Mauger; Hart had returned for the Heathens. Cradley would not be denied and led by 15-point maximums from Brown and Hart – they ran riot over Newcastle. Johnny Edwards repaid the faith that Roy Moreton had placed in him by scoring 13 terrific points, Derek Timms rode heroically to score 8, and Bastable and Totney never faltered, scoring 6 points apiece. Even Joe Westwood managed to get amongst the scorers as the Heathens lifted the Cup, beating the Diamonds 109-82 on aggregate.

Cradley finished off their League campaign with a home win against Exeter and then, as a special end-of-season treat, they took on National League Coventry. This was the first ever visit to Dudley Wood by a National League team, and the Heathens were strengthened by the inclusion of Eric Boocock and Jimmy Squibb.

The Cradley fans were delighted at the opportunity of seeing stars of the calibre of Nigel Boocock, Ron Mountford and Jim Lightfoot, and were even more delighted as Cradley came out on top, 49-47. The brilliant Nigel Boocock, in his first appearance at Dudley Wood, scorched to an untroubled 15-point maximum.

Another season had come to a close. Under-strength Cradley had a very undistinguished League campaign, finishing ninth from fifteen – rivals Wolverhampton had won the title – but for a team that had shown such indifferent League form, the silverware cabinet was bursting at the seams with the Knockout Cup, the Midland Cup and the Dudley/Wolves Trophy.

The incredible Ivor Brown had topped the League averages again with an unbelievable 11.5 points (as had Ove Fundin in the National League) over Jimmy Squibb, George Hunter and Ivan Mauger. All in all it had been a successful season, marred only, as everyone's was, by the untimely death at Edinburgh of one of speedway's greatest ever riders – the wonderful Peter Craven.

11

BROWN'S MAUGER PROBLEM
1964

The close season between 1963 and 1964 was a winter of discontent. An all-out war was developing between the Provincial League promoters and the Speedway Control Board. While the Provincial League was thriving, the National League, although boasting the top riders in the world, had lost Southampton and was down to a mere six teams. The Provincial League promoters felt, and had done for some time, that they had not been given a fair crack of the whip by the SCB and demanded an enquiry into the workings of the Board, but none was forthcoming. The Control Board instead gave an ultimatum – amalgamation.

The National League promoters let it be known right from the start that they would not be letting any of their star riders go, in order to re-distribute the strength throughout the proposed new League. Although the Provincial League had many emerging stars – Eric Boocock, Charlie Monk, Colin Pratt and Ivan Mauger, amongst others – these riders were clearly not in the class of the likes of Fundin and Briggs, so the Provincial League rejected the proposal. After all, it was the National League that needed the Provincial League, not the other way around.

In 1963, the top riders in the NL had been Fundin, Briggs, Bjorn Knutsson, Ronnie Moore and Peter Craven, and racing was run on a handicap basis. The five mentioned all had to start twenty yards behind the starting gate. Most of the second strings started from ten yards back, and the lesser lights went off scratch. The top stars were always against this, failing to see any justice in a system that penalised them for their undoubted talent.

Moore had already returned to New Zealand mid-season, Peter Craven had been tragically killed at the end of the season, and Fundin and Briggs had threatened retirement. Fearing that the National League might collapse, the SCB looked to the Provincial League for support and as the 1964 season approached, no compromise had been reached. On the eve of the season, the unrelenting Control Board issued a statement saying that any rider riding in the Provincial League would be 'black' and would not be issued with a licence. Obviously, all Provincial League tracks would be unlicensed.

Some riders took the view 'So what?' They were on a nice little earner in the Provincial League and had no further aspirations, so why should they need to be licensed? Others took the opposing view and were reticent, especially the ones who rode on the Continent. The season got underway with some riders absent from their team's line-up, and Cradley's team was no exception.

Roy Moreton was reappointed as team manager, and the first problem that he had to deal with was Harry Bastable's retirement. To say that Harry would be sorely missed would be an understatement, for he was Mr Cradley Heath Speedway. The Heathens owed him a great debt – it was he alone in 1960 that turned Cradley into a 'serious' outfit. He had shown them the way and his leadership had been an inspiration to them all.

There was no better team-man in speedway than Harry, but he had more than that – he had charisma. Even though he was a star, he always had his feet planted firmly on the ground, and, although Ivor Brown was undoubtedly the top Heathen, Harry had just as many fans. Brown always remained rather aloof off track, but Bastable was 'one of the boys', always prepared to share a laugh, a joke and a fag with the fans, and he was the life and soul of the many functions that he attended. Yes, Brown was worshipped but Bastable was genuinely loved. But now, at thirty-five, Harry wanted to leave Dudley Wood to spend more time at his successful motorbike business in nearby Blackheath, and Cradley had no option but to wish him 'Good luck'.

A comeback by Ivor Davies looked unlikely so, during the winter, Cradley made two useful signings in Eric Hockaday and Glynn Chandler, who, Morris Jephcott assured the supporters, had cost a fortune. Eric was a thirty-three year old Londoner, who had made quite an impression in his first year in the Provincial League with Rayleigh. He moved to Exeter the following year, but never quite got to grips with the County Ground circuit and moved on to become a valuable member of the Stoke Potters. The Sun Street Stadium had closed at the end of 1963, so Cradley snapped him up. Tiny Glynn Chandler had been signed from Trevor Redmond's St Austell after they had also closed. Glynn had come on in leaps and bounds in 1963, and his spectacular style was reckoned to make him a clear favourite with the fans.

Cradley's first matches were challenges, which was just as well as their opening match at Exeter saw Brown, Hart, Hockaday and Chandler all sitting on the fence, unsure of what move to make in the PL/SCB dispute. So what was Cradley's answer to this? They called back Harry Bastable! The Heathens lost, but got their revenge five nights later at Dudley Wood. By that time, only Hockaday was missing from the squad and, after watching the match from the terraces, he too signed his contract directly afterwards. John Edwards fell in heat twelve and became Cradley's first casualty of the season; after only two matches, things were already looking bad for Harry Bastable's retirement.

Further challenge matches at Sheffield and Wolverhampton saw the Heathens lose by small margins, and Brown claimed a new track record on his first visit of the season to Monmore Green. The following night, Cradley were hosts to Wolves who were still in the process of getting their team together, due to the dispute and Graham Warren's retirement. The visitors featured Ivan Mauger in their line-up as a guest, as they had at Monmore the previous night. Ivor beat Ivan in that match and also at Cradley, but in the scratch race final, Brown fell whilst challenging Mauger. He was allowed a re-run, and the same thing happened again. One sensed a little needle creeping into their encounters.

Programme cover from 21 March 1964.

Programme cover from 31 October 1964.

1964 team line-up. From left to right: John Hart, Eric Hockaday, Frank Holmes, Ivor Brown (on machine), Roy Moreton (manager), George Major, Alan Totney, Glyn Chandler. (Speedway Star)

The challenge matches continued with a narrow win over Sheffield at Dudley Wood in which Cradley had their second casualty when manager Moreton fell in the pits and broke his ankle! Brown scored his second maximum of the season, but by that time most of the attention had turned to Alan Totney who was going like a locomotive. John Hart had started to find his feet after a slow start, and Chandler and Hockaday were settling down. Harry was plugging in some solid scores, but the Heathens still had a problem at reserve where Derek Timms was struggling. Cradley reverted back to their system of the reserve being the winner of a pre-match run-off, the result of which would see one of Ron Cooper, Frank Holmes or Timms in the squad.

In early April, the serious stuff started with the Southern League matches. The Heathens got off to a blinding start, beating both Long Eaton and Newport at home and away before being pulled up sharply and losing to Poole by 4 points at Dudley Wood. By this time, Brown, Hart and Totney were all scoring well, as was Frank Holmes from his extended run at reserve.

At the beginning of May, Bastable was granted his wish and he retired. The ruling was that guest riders were allowed to be used in Southern League matches, so the Heathens plumped for Charlie Monk home and away against Wolverhampton (who were still using Mauger). In their first match at Monmore without Harry, Cradley crashed to a 50-28 defeat, Brown scoring only 2 points. He was hampered all night by engine troubles, and even trusty mechanic and long-time friend Les Widdowson could not prevent Ivor from having his worst meeting ever at the Wolves' den. Mauger scored a faultless maximum in the return at Dudley Wood, but the Heathens managed to win 41-37.

Since Bastable's departure, things had quickly taken a turn for the worse. Totney's form, due to a few tumbles and machine problems, had nose-dived, and Glynn Chandler had gone right off the boil, blowing two motors and a whole lot of confidence into the bargain. Even Frank Holmes seemed to have taken two steps backward and was rarely scoring.

The second week in May saw Cradley slump to their biggest defeat since the formation of the Provincial League. They scored only 18 points at Exeter to the Falcons' 60, no Heathen winning a single race, and two days later they were hammered at Poole 50-28. 'Kick 'em when they're down' the man said, and that's just what Johnny Edwards did. He was pronounced fit, said 'Thanks very much' and promptly shot off to Wimbledon.

Ivor Brown and Ivan Mauger. (Speedway Star)

George Major. (Speedway Post)

The Heathens were due to meet Sunderland a few days later in a League match (no guests allowed) so the management came up with an idea – ask Harry Bastable back! Harry could never refuse his beloved Heathens. He had enjoyed his two week-long retirement and, no doubt fully refreshed, he obliged with 9 points as Cradley won at Dudley Wood by 10 points. The Heathens began their defence of the Knockout Cup two nights later at Cradley when they just beat Edinburgh by 6 points. They might even have been held to a draw if Monarchs' captain Doug Templeton had not decided to put Hart and Totney into the fence in the last heat to get himself excluded. At the end of the match, Harry Bastable retired – again.

Upon the departure of Edwards, the Cradley management looked for a replacement, and found one in twenty-five-year-old Norwich junior, George Major. George had enjoyed Provincial League success under Trevor Redmond's guidance at Neath and St Austell and made his debut for the Heathens at Hackney in the middle of May when he top-scored with 11 points. However, he was unable to save Cradley from defeat on that occasion. Meanwhile, a young Welshman by the name of Ivor Hughes had made his debut in the Opportunity Stakes at Dudley Wood and was looking like something a bit special.

Cradley entertained Newcastle in their next home meeting and won by 4 points; Hart beat Ivan Mauger in the match, but failed to repeat the performance in the Silver Sash Match Race. It was Mauger's only defeat of the night and he got the better of Brown on two occasions. It must be said, however, that in his determination to beat 'King Cradley', the Kiwi broke the tapes in heat seven and was promptly fined £1. Surely he had proved his supremacy over Brown once and for all. When the two riders clashed again in the Scratch Race final, Brown was brought to grief and was left to pick himself up off the floor as Mauger pulled away to claim another victory.

After a comfortable win at Dudley Wood against Middlesbrough, in which Brown and Major both scored maximums, Cradley went to Newcastle as a stronger team with the inclusion of George. The Diamonds were in contention for the League Championship, and the mighty Mauger had hardly lost a race on his home track all season, but the Heathens lost by only 2 points – however, that was not the main talking point of the evening.

In heat nine, Mauger had beaten Brown in a fairly uneventful race, but heat twelve found them alongside one another again. This time Brown made the gate and, as Mauger attempted to pass him on the outside, Ivor took him wider and wider until both riders had virtually stopped as the safety fence loomed closer. By that time, Johnny Hart and Maurie Robinson had both overtaken them, but Brown recovered and re-took the lead, winning the race with a furious Mauger hot on his heels. A confrontation took place in the pits and both riders had to be forcibly restrained. Just one race later and the two were due to meet in the Silver Sash Match Race!

Mauger, by his own admittance, was out to get Brownie and the Heathen must have known it, for he was strangely subdued in the Match Race and never challenged his rival. The following is actually documented in Mauger's biography *Triple Crown Plus* under the chapter called 'The man I hated'. After both riders had qualified for the Scratch Race final, Mauger plotted his revenge. He was off gate one and Brown was next to him, off gate two – perfect. Before he left the pits, Mauger told team-mates Bill Andrew and Mike Watkin to 'keep out of the way'.

As the tapes went up, Mauger deliberately let Brown make the gate and coming out of the first turn, Ivan accelerated under Ivor and deliberately sent him into the fence. Brownie was carried off on a stretcher, taken to hospital and was out of the sport for four weeks with a badly gashed foot.

The feud was on. Unfortunately, it was a feud that Brown could not possibly win, for although Ivor had always shown dogged determination and was never a rider to back down on the track, Mauger had more – so much more. Ivan had a burning ambition that made him stop at absolutely nothing to achieve his ultimate goals. It took him to the very pinnacle of world speedway and put him in the record books as one of the greatest riders the world had ever seen. At twenty-five, Mauger was probably eight or so years younger than Brown, and as time was running out for 'The White Ghost of

Dudley Wood', Mauger was embarking on one of the greatest careers in the history of the sport.

Cradley were due to face Exeter in their next home League match and were not only without Brown, but Chandler too, he also having been injured at Newcastle. The Heathens may have thought that they had covered their problems to some extent when the prodigal Johnny Edwards, who had failed at Wimbledon, turned up at Dudley Wood. Cradley moved Derek Timms up a place and brought in Freddie Priest at reserve, but they had not bargained for another casualty as Totney crashed out of the meeting in heat five, courtesy of Alan Cowland.

Alan sustained two broken ribs to add to his already injured leg. It was too much for the Heathens and they lost by 4 points. Major and Hart scored well, and Eric Hockaday responded marvellously, being beaten only by the Falcon's top-scoring Jimmy Squibb. Even so, the bottom end looked perilously weak, with Edwards lacking confidence after having the stuffing knocked out of him in the National League, so the management had a great idea – to ask Harry Bastable back yet again!

Harry had been retired a whole month by then, and was probably a little rusty when at Dudley Wood a week later, the Heathens faced a very strong Hackney team led by Colin Pratt, Roy Trigg and Len Silver. Harry scored 5 points in the match, but it was not enough to save Cradley from a 6-point defeat. Moreton had dropped Timms and Priest and had brought in Ivor Hughes and Frank Holmes, but they managed only 1 point between them, and the majority of the Heathens' points came from Hart, Major and that man Eric Hockaday, who seemed to be wallowing in the extra responsibility.

A depleted Cradley completed their June fixtures by challenging Newport, both at home and away, for the Jenkins Trophy and predictably lost on aggregate. However, George Major gave the fans something to cheer about when he won the 100 Guineas Trophy at Long Eaton.

A heavy defeat at Sheffield opened the Heathens' July account and then a couple of days later, Ivor Brown made his comeback as Cradley played host to Edinburgh. Typically, he won his opening heat in the fastest time of the season, and rode to an untroubled maximum as the Heathens won by 43-35.

A week later, it was the Alan Hunt Trophy and this brought together Brown and his old friend Ivan Mauger. Before the meeting began, Brown approached Mauger in the changing rooms and some verbal abuse was exchanged. Unfortunately, the incident didn't stop there and they ended up fighting on the floor before the rest of the riders separated them. The trouble that would undoubtedly spill over onto the track during the meeting never happened however – in fact they never met. Brown was leading in heat one when he hit a greasy patch and fell off. Jack Kitchen was following close behind, too close to lay his bike down, and he hit Brown, putting both men in hospital. One meeting back and Brownie was out again! Ivan Mauger went on to win the meeting with a 15-point maximum.

With Ivor out and Alan Totney back, Cradley lost at Long Eaton but beat them a few nights later at Dudley Wood in the Knockout Cup, led by top-scoring Harry Bastable. By this time, the Heathens were languishing at the foot of the League table, and Totney – fed up with his equipment, his injuries and his form – was threatening retirement. It

Alan Totney. (Speedway Post)

was indeed the low point of the Heathens' season, and even though a surprise draw at Middlesbrough did little for team spirit, it did lift them above Glasgow in the League.

The Dudley/Wolves Trophy was the next obstacle to overcome and Cradley surprised a strong Wolverhampton outfit by drawing on aggregate and sharing the trophy, thanks to some vintage Bastable in the Dudley Wood leg.

August saw the Heathens display new-found confidence as they beat Poole and Hackney in their next two home matches, inspired by some more vintage Bastable. They visited Newport with renewed hope, but as number one (Ivor Brown) came back, number two was out, as John Hart became a casualty in his first race and Cradley lost by 18 points. At the end of the month, Morris Jephcott surprisingly announced his departure from Cradley Heath.

The next few matches saw an upturn in Cradley's form, and they were losing away matches by just a handful of points. Hart had returned, and Totney had decided to stick it out. However, a big test was imminent as the Heathens had drawn the newly crowned League Champions Newcastle in the Knockout Cup semi-final at Dudley Wood.

As it happens, the match itself was a bit of an anti-climax. It was always going to be about the Brown/Mauger saga – the two were only programmed to meet each other once in the match, but the awaited confrontation never took place. In that particular race, Mauger suffered an engine failure and Brown went on to win, as he did all of his races in fact, and the Heathens went into the final, beating the Diamonds 54-42.

One week later, on 25 September, the first leg of the final took place at Newport and Cradley suffered a double blow, losing the match by 20 points and also losing George Major with leg injuries that ended his season. The Heathens spent the next few weeks trying to stay off the bottom of the League table. Following Major's injury, Cradley contacted Glynn Chandler, who had been dropped at the beginning of September, only to be told that he would no longer be riding in 1964, so they brought in young Coventry junior Matt Mattocks, and he made his debut in early October.

Cradley's last League match was at home against Glasgow and the result would determine who would take the 'wooden spoon'. Hart, Brown and (surprisingly) Totney made sure that it was the Tigers.

24 October at Dudley Wood saw the Heathens with a mountain to climb in the second leg of the Knockout Cup final. Despite stirring performances by all of the team – Brown (15), Edwards (13), Hart (12), Bastable (7), Hockaday (5), Totney (5) and Mattocks (0) – the Heathens could not quite pull it off. After winning the match 57-39, they lost the Cup on aggregate by a mere 2 points, a result that would no doubt have been different had George Major been riding.

It had been decided to re-run the Dudley/Wolves Trophy at the end of the season, and Cradley lost both home and away, typifying what had been a diabolical season for them. Their injury record had been appalling, they had lost the Knockout Cup and they had finished tenth out of twelve in the League.

Ivor Brown had inevitably topped the averages with 10.65 points, but he had fallen to third place in the Provincial League Riders' averages behind Ivan Mauger (who had finished with an unbelievable 11.92) and Charlie Monk. It was a measure of how the standard of rider in the Provincial League had improved. Ivor had won no individual trophies for the first time in three years, and had spent time out injured, partly because of a stupid feud.

Johnny Hart had looked even better than the year before, although his average had stayed the same, but his second place in the team had gone to lanky George Major, who had been a huge success and averaged 9.38 points Eric Hockaday responded when the chips were down, but as soon as the injured riders came back, his form went into decline. Harry Bastable deserved a medal – period. Johnny Edwards had been disappointing and Glynn Chandler had been very disappointing. Poor old Alan Totney, after starting like a champion, finished up totally disillusioned, very sore indeed, and thinking seriously about the future. Incredibly, only once in the season had Cradley been able to field their strongest team.

Newcastle won the League Championship, Ivan Mauger won the Provincial League Riders' Championship – and Harry Bastable retired.

12

A BRUTAL BAPTISM
1965

The year 1965 was a milestone in British speedway history, for it saw the birth of the highly successful British League (BL). The sport could not have survived another 1964, when the bitterness and wrangles that continued throughout the year threatened to destroy it. The winter saw a huge summit where views and grievances were aired and a compromise was finally reached. It was agreed that there would be one big League with eighteen teams, of which Cradley Heath would be one. Handicapping would be abolished, and the only non-Commonwealth riders allowed to compete would be residents, such as Olle Nygren.

A new organisation was formed – the British Speedway Promoters Association (BSPA) – and they were to oversee the new League. Team strengths were obviously where the success or failure of the League would lie, and much time was spent in trying to distribute riders around the tracks that were under-strength. As expected, the old National League would not let go of their stars, so the likes of Coventry kept Nigel Boocock, Ron Mountford and Jim Lightfoot, and Oxford kept Arne Pander, Ron How and Jimmy Gooch. This being the case, amalgamation would certainly not bring equality.

A situation arose whereby all of the riders that were available could not find team places, so a 'pool' was formed that would 'hold' these riders. If a team lost a rider through injury or retirement, then they could draw a rider from the 'pool', and with team strengths to be reviewed on 15 May, any team found to be under-strength could likewise draw from the 'pool'.

With all that sorted out, the riders threatened a strike on the eve of the season. They found their terms of 22s 6d a start, £1 per point, and £8 maintenance unacceptable, and the BSPA found themselves in their first dispute before the season had even begun. However, it was all settled amicably, and the Heathens' fans were able to look forward to seeing some of the great world speedway stars appear at Dudley Wood, as Cradley Heathens were elevated to the finest speedway League in the world.

The Board had decided that Cradley, with the same line-up as 1964, were strong enough, especially since Harry Bastable had decided to give it another go. So, with Roy Moreton again at the helm, they opened the season with the first ever British League match at Coventry. In front of the biggest Brandon crowd for ten years, the Heathens went down 31-47. No Cradley rider won a race, but Brown did score

1965 programme cover.

1965 team line-up. From left to right: Eric Hockaday, Tim Bungay, John Hart, Ron Cooper, Leo McAuliffe, Matt Mattocks, Chris Julian, George Major. (Speedway Star)

double figures. Bastable had clearly regained his enthusiasm for the sport, for when he got stuck in a traffic jam on his way to the stadium, he pulled his car over, got changed into his leathers and hitched a lift to the track from a passing motor-cyclist, arriving minutes before the start of the match! After the match, Johnny Edwards (the yo-yo man) decided to return to Wimbledon, leaving the Heathens a man short.

Six nights later Cradley lost by 10 points at Monmore Green in a challenge match against an impressive Wolves side that included young Aussie sensations Jim Airey and Gordon Guasco. The Heathens won the return the following night at Dudley Wood, Brown getting into the swing of things with a paid maximum and George Major scoring double figures.

The next match was Cradley's first British League home match, and they were forced to face Hackney Hawks without 'flu-ridden George Major. They were, however, fielding their replacement for Edwards – the flying Cornishman, Chris Julian.

Twenty-eight-year-old Chris had made his speedway debut at Exeter in 1959 and rode for Bristol the following year in the Provincial League, under the tutelage of Trevor Redmond. The next few years saw him at Plymouth and St Austell, where he rode with George Major and Glynn Chandler. When the Gulls closed, he moved to Glasgow, where, although he had aspired to heat-leader, the 500-mile trip to home meetings had finally got the better of him and he asked for a transfer. Consequently, he became a Heathen. Chris was a no-nonsense rider, a great trier and an out-and-out tearaway, whose antics on the track were known to have upset opponent and team-mate alike. At any rate, he opened his account with 7 points as Cradley beat an 'out of sorts' Hackney by 20 points, Brownie scoring his second maximum.

The Heathens next found themselves away and then at home to Swindon, who boasted World Champion Barry Briggs, vastly experienced Mike Broadbanks and the very talented Martin Ashby. The first race at Blunsdon was a bit of an anti-climax as Briggs and Brown lined up in opposition, only to both suffer engine failures. Ivor did get the better of Broadbanks, however, and spoiled his maximum in heat twelve. A very solid Cradley performance saw them beat ex-National League Robins by 2 points, Julian leading the assault with 9 points. The following night at Dudley Wood, the Heathens won again by 40-38, but this time Briggs' equipment did not let him down, and he scorched through the meeting unbeaten. Cradley's top score was again 9, and this time it was Johnny Hart.

The matches pointed out an interesting aspect though. Whilst the ex-NL teams had retained their star riders, they had done so at the expense of the rest of the team, having had to settle for inexperienced or junior riders to fill the gaps. In the case of Swindon, at Blunsdon their bottom four had scored only 7 points between them, and at Dudley Wood only 5 points. So, maybe the likes of Cradley, who had the ability to score through the ranks, could do well against the big boys. As if to prove a point, two nights later in the Hammers Trophy at West Ham, ex-Provincial League Charlie Monk took the trophy ahead of Nigel Boocock and Reg Luckhurst.

In the middle of April, with things looking rosy for the Heathens, the BSPA decided to throw a spanner in the works and declared Cradley to be too strong. They decreed that they should release Alan Totney – to Newcastle! Totney rightly said that if he could not ride for his native Cradley, then he did not want to ride for anyone else, and promptly retired. The Heathens then recalled Ivor Hughes from the second halves, but in their next match, when they were defeated at Hackney, they lost Eric Hockaday with a suspected broken thigh.

After beating Long Eaton at Dudley Wood, Cradley were third

Eric Hockaday. (Speedway Post)

in the British League after six League matches – the premier League in world speedway. The news was that Eric had not broken his thigh and, with a bit of luck, would miss only a handful of matches. Brown was piling up the points, and so was George Major. Hart, although finding it tough away from home, was looking better all the time at Dudley Wood, and new boy Julian was putting in some gritty performances. The tail end was a cause for concern, with Bastable finding the pace a little too hot, and Ivor Hughes was understandably outclassed at this level, as was Matt Mattocks.

The Heathens went comfortably into May, losing Mattocks with a bruised kidney but regaining the services of Hockaday, and lost narrowly at Oxford, who boasted the most powerful heat leader trio in the League. Brown and Major scored a brilliant 5-1 over 'Great Dane' Arne Pander, again proving that all-round scoring ability was better than three stars and four 'lemons'.

The next home encounter against Newcastle was a thriller, but not because of Ivan Mauger – he had broken his ankle at the start of the season and this probably helped to defuse the situation with Ivor Brown. Ivan had been replaced with the very lively Brian Brett, and the Heathens found themselves 6 points down with two races left. Hart paired up with Brown in heat twelve to beat Brian Craven and Ken Sharples, and in the final race Brown and Major did the same to Peter Kelly and Brett to win a thrilling match by 2 points and maintain their third place in the League. Brown found himself fourth in the League averages with a very creditable 10.3 points.

Cradley continued the month battling away, barely losing at West Ham, beating Belle Vue at Dudley Wood and losing by only 2 points at Edinburgh, but their luck was about to take a turn for the worse. The Heathens had somewhat prematurely let Ivor Hughes move on to Exeter and therefore gave a chance to ex-Norwich rider John Debbage. In their next League match, against Wolverhampton, George Major crashed in the opening heat and was taken to hospital with facial abrasions, concussion and knee damage. Cradley won the home match but paid dearly for it, losing their second-best rider.

It was obvious that George's injuries would keep him out for some time, so the management applied to the BSPA and were given thirty-two-year-old Welshman Leo McAuliffe, who had been languishing in the 'pool'. Leo was a rider of quite some experience and achievement, having found success with National League Wimbledon in the early 1960s. 1963 saw him in the World Championship final and also representing Great Britain in the World Team Cup final, so he was hardly without credentials. Unfortunately, life in the 'pool' had left Leo rusty, but even before he began to race for Cradley, disaster befell the Heathens.

Wimbledon were hosting their annual 'Internationale' meeting on Bank Holiday Monday, 7 June. It was, as always, a star-studded affair, featuring the best riders in the world. They were even flying in the top Swedes – Bjorn Knutsson, Ove Fundin and Gote Nordin to ride in just this one event. Ivor Brown had been given the honour of an invitation to ride in the event, confirming that he was acknowledged as one of the best riders in the sport. Over 400 Cradley supporters made the trip to

Chris Julian. (Speedway Post)

London to cheer Ivor on in the biggest meeting of his life, and they wouldn't have to wait long to do so as he went out in heat one. It was all over in seconds. As Brown hit the first bend, Fundin, who was never one for on-track pleasantries, cut across the Heathen, forcing him to clip the Swede's back wheel. Both Ivor and his machine crashed heavily into the fence, causing awful injuries to his spine and posterior. He was immediately rushed to St George's hospital at Tooting, where it was confirmed that he would not race again for weeks. Cradley Heath were left without their Golden Boy.

The day before, Harry Bastable had shown the youngsters that he still knew a thing or two by winning the first round qualifier of the World Championship at Kings Lynn, when his 15-point maximum won him the £10 cheque. Inexplicably, in the light of what happened the following day, Harry rode at Cradley when the Heathens beat Exeter the following weekend, and then retired.

George Major immediately made a comeback, maybe prematurely, but the man was made of stern stuff and he top-scored with 13 points as Cradley lost by 6 points at Newcastle. The Heathens had promoted Ron Cooper from the juniors to reserve, and he was understandably out of his league, as was John Debbage, who failed to make any impact whatsoever. Julian was riding hard and getting little back to show for it, and McAuliffe was finding it difficult to get back into the swing of things. With Hockaday rarely scoring half-a-dozen, Cradley were relying heavily on Hart and Major for their returns. Their seventh place in the League was looking precarious.

Once again they dived into the 'pool' and emerged with Tim Bungay, who had recently retired from Exeter. Tim proved not to be the answer, however, as the Heathens were thrashed at Dudley Wood by high-flying Coventry. They lost Major when he fell in his first outing, aggravated his knee injury and joined Ivor Brown on the sidelines. It completely knocked the stuffing out of Cradley, and the team spirit collapsed. After losing heavily at Edinburgh, they visited Halifax and set a record for the biggest defeat ever in the British League, losing by 62-16. At The Shay, the

Heathens turned out in dirty leathers and filthy body colours and put in a performance to match when they gave points away on a plate.

The lack of spirit became contagious and spread to the management as Cradley's next home match, a win against lowly Edinburgh, took nearly two hours to complete. It continued at Newport when Hockaday and McAuliffe didn't show up until 8.00 p.m., and Hart left the stadium after two rides, totally dissatisfied with starting procedures.

Wolverhampton visited Dudley Wood and predictably knocked the Heathens out of the Knockout Cup competition, despite a fine maximum from Hart. Cradley also lost their next two matches, with McAuliffe and Bungay absent through illness. The Heathens were a club in crisis and were plummeting down the League table. Once again they asked for assistance, only to be told that the 'pool' had run dry.

However, thirty-four-year-old New Zealander Goog Allen had become surplus to requirements at Newcastle and Cradley snapped him up. Goog, like Bungay, was not the answer to the Heathens' problems, for it would have taken Barry Briggs himself to drag Cradley out of this quagmire. In a match at Dudley Wood against West Ham, Hart again walked out, claiming that conditions were too bad to take part, and the Heathens received another trouncing.

Major made a comeback to try and help Cradley to win the Dudley/Wolves Trophy, but he was obviously suffering and his efforts were to no avail. The

Heathens travelled to Long Eaton and became the first team in thirteen matches NOT to beat the Archers. After four months, Ivor Brown returned to Dudley Wood and Cradley beat the Poole Pirates. He rode to the fastest time of the night in heat two, but he was in constant pain, riding heavily strapped up, and although he scored only 7 points, his mere presence in the pits inspired the Heathens to their first win in 11 matches. His influence continued as Cradley won the Iron and Steel Trophy against Newport, but in mid-October he finally

John Hart. (Speedway Post)

succumbed to the pain and sat out the rest of the season; a season that had promised to propel him to super-stardom, but instead had almost left him crippled for life.

George Major continued to ride bravely through the pain barrier and represented the Heathens in the first British League Riders' Championship at Belle Vue, but he crashed out on the first bend of the first heat, aggravating his injuries and bending his bike.

There is little to say about the remainder of Cradley's 1965 season. They lost their last six League matches and only their earlier success kept them above Edinburgh and Long Eaton in the British League table. Brown finished the season with an average of 10.00, Hart 8.35, and Major 7.45.

One could almost hear the sighs of relief from riders and supporters alike as the last race of 1965 was run and the Heathens hobbled back to the changing rooms, a broken bunch. The riders that were not suffering from injuries were suffering from broken spirits. It had been a brutal, bloody baptism for the Heathens.

13

A DEATH IN THE FAMILY
1966

Cradley underwent quite a few changes in the close season leading up to their 1966 campaign. Goog Allen went back to Newcastle, Tim Bungay retired, as did Leo McAuliffe (only to re-emerge at Oxford), but the biggest surprise was the departure of John Hart and George Major, two of the Heathens' top scorers in 1965.

The first Hart heard about it was when he received a phone-call just prior to the season getting underway to say that terms had been agreed with Sheffield and he was to ride at Owlerton in 1966. Hart was apparently taken aback by this news, until he was further informed that George Major would accompany him and, as they both worked together, it seemed to suit the pair of them and off they went.

Replacements came in all shapes and sizes. There was Kid Bodie from Long Eaton who, at twenty-three, was surely the right age to develop into a prolific scorer at Cradley. In fact, he had been the Heathens' mascot way back in 1952, leading them out onto the Dudley Wood track on a scaled-down speedway bike specially built by his father, Howard Cole.

Kid Bodie had begun his speedway career at Wolverhampton in 1961 and rode under an alias to prevent his mother and the headmaster of Wolverhampton Grammar School, where he was a student, learning of his speedway activities. He moved on to Stoke the following year, and then Long Eaton in 1964. He was becoming a more accomplished rider with every season that passed, and Cradley promoter Alan Martin and manager Moreton swooped to sign him in the hope that he would progress into a future star.

The next 'new' man would surely not progress into a future star, for how much future a thirty-eight-year-old could have in speedway was questionable, and that's how old Chum Taylor was when he arrived at Dudley Wood. Chum had become Australian Champion in the winter and had represented the Aussies at international level many times, including World Team Cup appearances. He had been a World finalist in 1960 and had been a useful member of the Oxford and Southampton teams in the old National League, but he had stayed in his home country in 1965. With Taylor's experience, Cradley were looking for him to settle down into scoring from day one.

In a part of the deal with Sheffield, Cradley acquired the enigmatic Clive Featherby. Clive had finished the previous season second to Jack Kitchen in the Tigers' averages, and on his day could beat the very best that the sport had to offer. He had, you will recall, briefly ridden for the Heathens back in the old Provincial League days, so he certainly knew the track, but there was a problem – Clive didn't want to come to

1966 programme cover.

1966 team line-up. From left to right, back row: Chris Julian, Clive Featherby, Ted Flanaghan (manager), Rick France (guest), Ivor Hughes. Front row: Matt Mattocks, Ivor Brown, Chum Taylor. (Speedway Star)

Cradley Heath. He wanted a move to his local track, Kings Lynn, who were making their debut in the British League. His request was turned down and so Featherby reluctantly became a Heathen, but he came with a reputation of being difficult if things did not go his way.

The transfer business with Sheffield was still incomplete when the League programme commenced, and as the Heathens were once again involved in the curtain raiser at Brandon, Hart took his place in the squad for the last time. Coventry beat the Heathens convincingly, 50-28, with Hockaday and Bodie being Cradley's only race winners, but young Ivor Hughes, back from Exeter, impressed by scoring 4 points. Brown top-scored for the Heathens with 8 points, Bodie 7, Hart 3, Hockaday 3, Julian 2, and Taylor 1. The following Friday, Cradley lost by 10 points at Monmore Green, where Brown was at his best, scoring 14 points, but Featherby could muster only a single point on his debut, pulling out after only one ride. Featherby missed the next four meetings for the Heathens and they were allowed a guest facility for him.

Long Eaton's young hotshot, Ray Wilson, made two appearances as Cradley were thrashed by Coventry in their first home match, and they were given an even bigger caning at Swindon, but at least by now Chum Taylor had moved his scoring up into the middle order. He went on to top-score in the next match at Dudley Wood as visitors Newport were beaten, but he was unsuccessful in his challenge for Gote Nordin's Silver Sash. It was a fine performance from the Heathens since they were without Kid Bodie, who had contracted measles and was to miss a further two matches. Ever-ready junior

Ron Cooper was called into battle.

After losing at Poole, Cradley's next match was at Wimbledon. Clive Featherby actually turned up, explaining that the printing firm for which he worked (most of the riders had other jobs in those dark days) had asked him to make a delivery in London and so he had turned up to ride. Clive actually gave a good account of himself, but his 6 points could not save the Heathens from defeat. He did, however, seem to resign himself to the fact that his wish to join Kings Lynn would not be granted, and so he settled down with Cradley. He never regained his Sheffield form, but at least he showed up.

Kid Bodie returned to Dudley Wood in mid-April and probably wished that he hadn't, as the Heathens crashed to Poole. Further misery was around the corner for him when, at the end of the month, he crashed in the Midland Riders' Championship qualifying round at Monmore Green, damaging his knee and putting himself on the injured list as opposed to the sick list. Ivor Brown was also injured in the same meeting, but the rugged Mr B missed only a single match before returning.

After ten matches, Cradley had won only once. Bodie was out, but Brown was giving it his best as always, although he rode in constant pain due to the injuries that he sustained in 1965. Julian had settled into mid-order scoring, but Featherby's heart was not in it and Taylor was finding that his vast experience was not enough to reap the points that Cradley expected from him. Ivor Hughes was proving to be the jewel in the crown with some gritty performances, but how much could the Heathens expect from him in his first full term? The Welsh plumber was certainly keen enough, and had even purchased a new ESO machine in order to enhance his chances in the highly competitive League.

With juniors Cooper and Mattocks in the team, it was obvious that Cradley were under-strength. They were at the foot of the League table and looked like staying there, so they applied for permission to sign another heat-leader. There is nothing quite like starting at the top, so Alan Martin approached World Champion Bjorn Knutsson, only to be told that Bjorn, although he quite fancied the idea of racing in the British League in 1967, would be staying in his native Sweden in 1966. Living legend Ronnie Moore was contacted in New Zealand but had to refuse as his 'Wall of Death' show was booked up until February 1967.

The Heathens began their May home matches with their best performance of the year so far, a 48-30 win over Belle Vue, in which Chris Julian gave a breathtaking display and helped himself to his first maximum in Cradley colours. It did, however, lead to Aces' Cyril Maidment having a word with the ebullient Cornishman about the tactics that he employed to achieve the said maximum.

Defeats away and at home at the hands of Wolverhampton in the Midland Cup were a bitter pill for the Heathens' fans to swallow, but Brown was unbeaten at Monmore and dropped only a point at Cradley as the Heathens were relegated from the Cup competition.

A visit to Dudley Wood by Swindon saw Cradley scrape a 1-point victory, and they must have thought that they had found their elusive heat-leader when Ivor Hughes popped up with 11 points from four rides and beat Martin Ashby into the bargain.

Hughes had been paired with Ivor Brown for some weeks , and Brownie must have been a good influence on the lad for he was improving in leaps and bounds. Against the Robins, it was the pupil who scored more points than the master, so Ivor Hughes challenged Barry Briggs for the Silver Sash. In heat one of the match, Ivor had finished ahead of Briggs, Barry suffering an engine failure, but in the match race, Briggo was not about to let the young upstart enhance his reputation any further at *his* expense and made a successful defence.

Ivor 'Two' struggled over the next few matches, as did all of the Heathens. They were all away fixtures and bore no fruit for Cradley as they languished at the foot of the League table. The number seven slot was usually filled by Ron Cooper, Matt Mattocks or Joe Weichlbauer, an Austrian-born naturalised Australian who had come over with Chum Taylor to try his luck, but apart from the odd point, none of these three made any impression.

The reason that Cradley had ridden so many matches away from home is that Dudley Wood had been staging their qualifying round of the World Championship (won by Ivor Brown), the Alan Hunt Trophy (won by Barry Briggs), followed by the British semi-final (won by Trevor Hedge). The last of these meetings saw the arrival of Ted Flanaghan as speedway manager at Cradley Heath. Roy Moreton found that his business had made it increasingly difficult for him to make the away meetings, so he handed over to ex-Oxford co-promoter Ted. Alan Martin carried on as stadium manager and business adminis-trator. One door opens and another one closes, and Eric Hockaday left for Sheffield.

Almost as expected, the Heathens got knocked out of the Knockout Cup in the first round. They were away at Hackney, but they nearly pulled off one of the upsets of the season, losing by only a single point. Cradley were without any guests as Howard Cole had made his comeback (Kid Bodie had decided to use his real name, no doubt hoping that it might change his luck). Brown, Julian, Taylor, Hughes and Featherby all rode like heroes to give the Hawks the fright of their lives.

Meanwhile, back at the ranch, Cradley had been featuring a young Netherton lad in the second halves – Mick Handley – and so had Wolverhampton. As Mick began to progress, Wolves claimed rights to him, but Cradley pointed out that Mick wanted to join the Heathens. After much debate, Cradley lost out on and Mick had to pay his penance at Monmore before returning to Dudley Wood in later years.

The Heathens lost their next three matches – two at home and the last against unfancied Kings Lynn. Any other team would have begun to lose their following by now, but the Cradley supporters were made of strong stuff, and week after week they turned out, trying to instill some fire into the Heathens' bellies.

Flanaghan reciprocated by painting the stadium. It was about all he could do because despite his efforts, he had not been able to find Cradley the other heat-leader that they so desperately needed. Brown was still capable of brilliance, but the constant pain had robbed him of his consistency. He was visiting a back specialist every week and only he will ever know what agonies he endured when the tapes went up and he threw his bike into the first bend. But Ivor Hughes was the name on everyone's lips at that time. He had top-scored for the Heathens twice in their previous three outings, and was going from strength to strength.

June began for Cradley with a visit to Monmore Green. Although the Wolves were in the top half of the League and the Heathens were rock bottom, the bitter rivalry between the two teams was undiminished. Wolves won by a comfortable margin, but in the final heat, Chris Julian put Aussie Gordon Guasco into the safety fence. Gordon waited for Chris to come round the track after the race and flung himself upon the Heathen. Blows were exchanged, and the pair had to be parted by track staff. Guasco was fined £5 for his outburst, and the fans were left wondering what would happen when the pugilists met the following night at Dudley Wood.

As it happens, very little occurred because as they lined up in opposition in heat ten, Guasco completely missed the gate as Julian fled away. So frustrated was the Wolves rider that he hurled his bike to the ground, regardless of the fact that the other three riders would be racing past that same spot just seconds later. He was promptly fined another £5. In the height of such drama, the results sometimes take second place so, for the record, Wolves won by 46-32 at Monmore and Cradley won 44-34 at Dudley Wood. Opponents weren't the only riders that Julian managed to upset. His main

Clive Featherby and Ivor Hughes. (Speedway Post)

Joe Weichlbauer. (Speedway Post)

problem was that he rode every race as though his very life depended upon it, so if it happened to be a team-mate that was in his way he would move them over. His pairing with Featherby never worked well, and one wonders why ever they were kept together for so long. In one match, Chris dived under Clive and took his footrest off, causing 'Feathers' to threaten immediate retirement!

Following the Wolves match, Cradley's form took a definite turn for the better, with Brown, Julian and Hughes all scoring well and Taylor showing his best form of the season. Featherby and Cole, who was still suffering with a damaged cartilage, were scoring between 5 and 7 points a match. The Heathens won their next two home meetings and lost by only 2 points at lowly Kings Lynn, when an engine failure by Featherby in the last heat undoubtedly cost them the match.

In the next match, against Wimbledon at Cradley Heath, Joe Weichlbauer fell victim to the Cradley jinx, falling and breaking his collarbone before the match in a run-off for the reserve spot. The Heathens narrowly lost the match and then moved on to Newcastle where an inevitable thrashing took place, Taylor being reprimanded by the referee for not trying. Just as the Cradley team spirit was about to dip, Ivor Hughes hit a patch of form that made him the most talked about rider in the British League.

It began at Dudley Wood against an unsuspecting Hackney, when he led the Heathens to victory with a faultless maximum. In the next home match, Cradley entertained the Swedish touring side, Vagarna, who were led by the peerless World Champion, Bjorn Knutsson. The Heathens, strengthened by the inclusion of Colin Pratt, won the match comfortably, and Hughes again top-scored with 10 points. Knutsson was superb, being unbeaten throughout the match, but in the Scratch Race final, even he had to take second place to Cradley's Welsh Wonder. The Heathens' fans had had little to cheer about in 1966, and they rejoiced in Hughes' emergence as the British League's new whizz-kid. Against Swindon at Dudley Wood, he was at it again, heading the pack with 10 points and leading the Heathens to victory. And then it was over, almost as quickly as it had begun.

Cradley's next home fixture was against Sheffield on 20 August and Ivor Hughes was unbeaten in three outings. In the final heat, he locked up and was run into by the Sheffield rider behind him. Ivor was rushed to Dudley Guest Hospital and at 3.00 a.m. the following Tuesday, he lost the fight for his life. Ivor Hughes was twenty-six years old. What had been a season of woe had turned into a season of unbelievable tragedy.

The rest of the season was academic. As the shock waves rippled through Dudley Wood, riders completed the term on automatic pilot and supporters quietly mourned their new star who had been so cruelly snatched from their midst at the height of his career.

Cole again fell foul of injury and Cradley used a number of guests to get them through to the eagerly awaited end of the season. Local lad Ken Wakefield was brought up through the ranks and rode the remainder of the season at reserve, Ron Cooper having retired following the death of his friend Hughes.

The Heathens lost the Dudley/Wolves Trophy, but the burden that they bore far outweighed the local rivalry, and Wolves challenged Cradley at Dudley Wood in September in a match from which the proceeds went to the 'Ivor Hughes Fund'. At a time like this in speedway, rivalry is never the issue and the riders without fail show their true character. When the match was first conceived, Wolves' Pete Jarman typically offered to ride for nothing.

Just before the end of the season, Chris Julian hit a purple patch and scored prolifically, but it was too late to lift Cradley from the bottom of the League table. Chum Taylor returned home before the League fixtures had been completed, and Ted Flanaghan, who had never given up his quest to find new riders, introduced twenty-two-year-old Swede, Tommy Bergqvist. Tommy rode in the Swedish League for Taxarna and came highly recommended by Olle Nygren. He showed promise in Cradley's last two meetings, whereas Clive Featherby finished as he had begun, walking out of the final match at Edinburgh after only a single outing. He epitomised what all of the Heathens must have felt at one time or another during this trying, tragic season.

14

THE RELUCTANT AUSTRALIAN 1967

There were major changes again at Dudley Wood after their nightmare season of 1966. Only two of the riders that had started the 1966 season were scheduled to be in the squad to begin the 1967 season – Ivor Brown, and Chris Julian. Howard Cole was also named, but he was completing a very successful winter season in New Zealand, where he had won the New Zealand Championship. Cradley looked forward to his return, more experienced and, presumably, full of confidence. So what of the rest?

Clive Featherby finally got his wish and moved to Kings Lynn, Chum Taylor remained in Australia, and, of course, Ivor Hughes was no longer with us. The Cradley management, who could never be accused of 'age discrimination', signed Jack Biggs from Newport. That is not to say that Jack was not a fine rider, but he had made his World final debut in 1950, and that gives an indication of how old the Australian veteran was. Again, nothing wrong with that, but Cradley surely should have been looking to re-build the team, and one wondered how much longer Biggsy could continue. At any rate, his pedigree was sound, having been an Australian international and one of the best riders in speedway at one time.

Graham Coombs had guested for Cradley in the midst of their troubles in 1966, and the likeable Kiwi was allocated to the Heathens in the close season. The twenty-seven-year-old had never seen eye to eye with the Newcastle management, so he was keen to join Cradley and they were pleased to have him. It came as no surprise to see Tommy Bergqvist in the side after his brief appearance at the end of 1966, and Tommy became the Heathens' first Swedish signing.

The last one was reckoned to be the 'biggie'. Cradley had done what many others had failed to do – they had signed Australian Jack Scott, on a two-year contract at that. In 1961, Jack was being hailed as a future world champion, but he left Bristol Bulldogs and returned home, evading all efforts to capture his signature. But now, at thirty-three, the Australian Champion was willing to return, and the team that he had chosen was Cradley Heathens. The Heathens were a strong team on paper, the strongest in the League according to the management committee, but this was Cradley Heath, where the form-book counted for nothing.

Cradley opened their campaign with a challenge match at Wolverhampton, fielding Ken Wakefield at reserve. With the abolishment of the 'no foreigners rule', Wolves had

9th MEETING - 20th May 1967
7.30 p.m.

CRADLEY HEATH SPEEDWAY

BRITISH SPEEDWAY LEAGUE
CRADLEY HEATH
v
SHEFFIELD
OFFICIAL PROGRAMME — PRICE NINEPENCE

1967 programme cover.

made a very astute signing in Swede Hasse Holmqvist, and he notched up an impressive maximum in his very first match, leading the Wolves to a comfortable win. Jack Scott top-scored for the Heathens with 8 points, which was quite impressive as he rode on borrowed bikes all night, his own being on a boat somewhere between Cradley Heath and Australia. The Cradley hoodoo was up and about right from the start in 1967, and in his last outing, Bergqvist broke a bone in his foot and was out for a month. Ivor Brown, once the scourge of Monmore, scored 4 points and one began to wonder if he would ever again score a maximum around his favourite track with the likes of Holmqvist present.

In the return at Dudley Wood the following night, the Heathens brought in Joe Weichlbauer, but a weakened Cradley lost by 4 points, mainly due to Holmqvist who, on his first look at the track, scored a 15-point maximum. But Brown pulled himself together and scored 12 points, Julian scored well, and Scott and Biggs on their home debut gave reasonable performances.

Cradley lost at Long Eaton, but their next match was a home fixture against Jackie Bigg's former club Newport, and the old campaigner responded with 13 points but it was not enough. Scott retired from the meeting after falling in his first race, and the Heathens, already without Bergqvist and Cole, lost by 8 points.

Before the next match at Sheffield, there was good news and bad news. The good news was that Jack Scott's bike had arrived at Southampton docks and he was driving down to collect it in time for the match. The bad news was that Howard Cole had arrived back in England, but a disagreement had arisen between himself and the Cradley management with regard to who should pay for his fare back home. Cole announced that he would not be donning the Cradley race jacket until the dispute had been settled in his favour. It was deadlock.

The Heathens lost heavily at Owlerton, but astride his own machine, Scott shone, scoring 12 points. He top-scored again with a brilliant 14 points against Poole at Dudley Wood, leading Cradley to a narrow victory. However, 'the strongest team in the League' was looking decidedly weak, and found themselves at the bottom of the League table once again.

At least it seemed that the Heathens had struck gold with Jack Scott. Battle-weary Ivor Brown was still the backbone of the team and was still scoring well, but Julian had so far failed to find the form that he displayed at the end of 1966. Apart from a couple of good scores, Biggs was struggling, Graham Coombes had not got going at all, and Ken Wakefield was finding the competition too much for his limited experience.

Bergqvist was still on the injured list and Cole had yet to put in an appearance. It was a situation reminiscent of the previous year. Cradley tried to put the pressure on Cole but he was adamant and they were unrelenting, so Howard put in a transfer request. Flanaghan approached the BSPA and applied for another rider, only to be told that whilst Cole was 'on the books', permission could not be granted.

The Heathens lost their next six matches, even with Bergqvist back in the side, and Jack Scott began to struggle just as Julian hit top form, scoring double figures at home and away. At Newcastle, Cradley came across a young Dane who was making his debut under the tutelage of Ivan Mauger – Ole Olsen scored 8 points against Cradley in his first ever British League match.

Toward the end of May, Jack Biggs announced his retirement after more than twenty years of racing – nice for Jack, but not so nice for the Heathens, who paid the penalty for signing a rider who was already in the twilight of his career. However, by this time, Bergqvist and Coombes were chipping in with some good scores, and if Scott had not been experiencing a bad run of machine troubles, Cradley could have started to climb

1967 team line-up. From left to right: Ken Wakefield, Alan Totney, Tommy Bergqvist, Ivor Brown, Chris Julian, Grahame Coombes, Brian Brett. (Speedway Star)

up the League ladder. Poor old Scotty had already blown two engines by the time the Heathens took on Oxford at Dudley Wood, and when he blew a third warming up for the match, it proved too much for Jack and he walked out of the meeting, leaving Cradley to struggle to a draw. His bad luck was not over, however, and in a Midland Riders qualifying round, Scott's engine died on him, throwing him to the ground and injuring his shoulder.

Howard Cole was transferred to Kings Lynn and, in early June, Cradley were given a replacement that they could be well pleased with – Brian Brett. Twenty-nine-year-old Brian looked a better bet altogether. He had topped the Newcastle averages in 1965 and that same year had finished in sixth place in the World final. He retired at the end of 1965 as his cleaning business had made it difficult for him to commute to Borough Park, but now, although undoubtedly a little rusty, he decided to give it a go as a Heathen.

He made his debut in a lively match at Dudley Wood when Cradley easily beat Exeter, and scored 4 points. In heat seven Brown nudged Falcons' veteran Jimmy Squibb into the fence, and upon his return to the pits, Squibby threatened to 'punch Brownie's head'. Jack Scott retired from the meeting after two outings, claiming that his shoulder injury was too painful to ride with. It was, in fact, the Australian Champion's last match for the Heathens, although they didn't know it at the time. Cradley scored just over 20 points at Newport, Graham Coombes getting nearly half of them, but the question on everyone's lips was 'Where's Jack Scott?'

The next couple of weeks saw the Heathens struggle, as they were forced to track youngsters such as Dave Schofield and Peter Wrathall to replace the missing Scott. It was a pity, because Coombes had found his feet, Brett was getting back into it, and Brown and Bergqvist were both scoring well. Toward the end of June, Jack Scott emerged to announce that he was going home. He had been staying with fellow Aussie rider Geoff Mudge and had sold all of his equipment in order to buy himself a return ticket and would be sailing in the next few days. The Cradley management pointed out that he had signed a two-year contract, and if he did not honour it, they would be forced to take action. Jack Scott left England two days later.

There is no doubt that Jack had had abysmal luck since his arrival on these shores. The first three months of the season had been a catalogue of blown motors and injuries, but those are misfortunes that many riders have had to endure and overcome. Scott was wrong to quit. Eric Hockaday returned to help out, but he scored only 5 points in as many matches and Cradley lost them all. In desperation (and I use that term in no derogatory manner to the rider concerned), the management approached Alan Totney. Alan, you may recall, had not ridden for two years and had been busy running his engineering company in neighbouring Old Hill. However, he never could say no to Cradley and agreed to sign up mid-term to make his debut in the British League.

Totney's arrival marked the departure of Hockaday, and Alan took a reserve berth alongside Ken Wakefield. By this time it was mid-July, and Brett had hit top form but Brown was going through a slump. Towards the end of the month, Julian again found his best form and beat Ove Fundin twice at Dudley Wood as Belle Vue Aces were

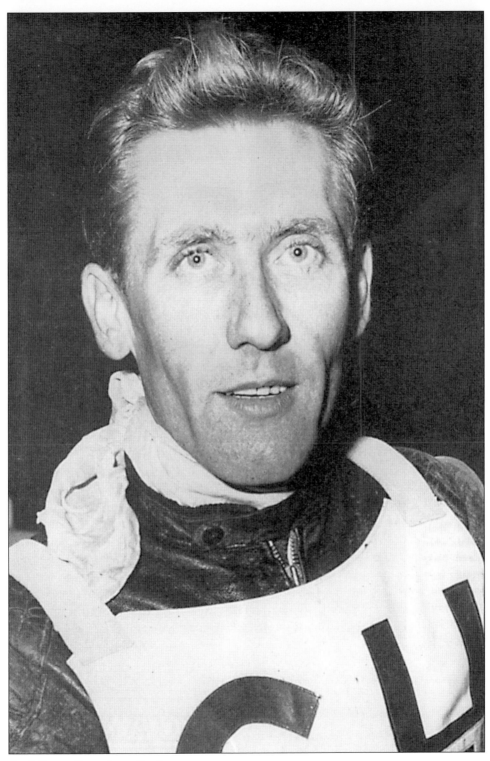

Jack Scott. (Speedway Post)

Brian Brett. (Speedway Star)   *Tommy Bergqvist.* (Speedway Star)

crushed. If only Julian, Brown, Brett, Coombes and Bergqvist could have clicked on the same night, Cradley would indeed have been formidable opposition. Every one of them had top-scored, and there was no way of knowing which one it was going to be, but some stout home performances had hauled them up over Kings Lynn in the League.

At the end of August, just when things seemed to be going their way at last, the Heathens lost Bergqvist with a broken collarbone and Coombes with a broken ankle. Both had seen the end of their speedway for 1967. Even so, Cradley visited Halifax and beat the Dukes by a point, thereby ending the Heathens record of 48 consecutive away League defeats. Peter Wrathall was recalled to fill the gap, and Cradley put up some creditable performances, due to the determined riding of Brett, Brown and Julian, as well as some eye-catching displays by twenty-seven-year-old Wakefield.

The Heathens ended another disappointing season in September, Brown missing a couple of meetings through injury and Julian still 'knocking 'em off'. They held onto their place above Kings Lynn in the League and Ivor Brown topped Cradley's averages with a mere 7.47 points, just ahead of Brian Brett. Brownie had once again held the team together in a season that had promised so much and had yielded so little.

15

THE END OF AN ERA
1968

For their 1968 campaign, Cradley were allocated two riders who – along with Brown, Julian, Coombes, Bergqvist, and Wakefield – should have made them the strongest outfit in the League (again!). The first acquisition was Bob Andrews, a London-born naturalized New Zealander who had risen to fame with Wimbledon in the early 1960s. Bob had appeared in four World finals, his best being in 1961 when he finished fifth. He had joined Wolverhampton in 1965, but returned in the winter and had since confined himself to domestic racing until Ted Flanaghan had persuaded him to join the Heathens for their 1968 season.

Cradley's other new face was a replacement for the retired Brian Brett, and Roy Trigg should have been more than adequate to fill Brian's shoes. Twenty-five-year-old Roy was one of the up-and-coming crop of young Englishmen that were emerging in the British League at that time. Triggy had had his fair share of clubs, starting with Wimbledon in the National League, before moving into the Provincial League with Poole and Hackney. Rider Control moved him on to Oxford in 1966, and Roy quickly established himself as their star rider. After returning from his second winter tour of Australia and New Zealand, he found that he had been allocated to Cradley Heath. Trigg arrived at Dudley Wood with a reputation as being one of the nicest men in speedway, and did much to enhance that reputation in the years that he spent as a Heathen.

Perhaps the most significant event in the sport during the winter was the formation of a Second Division in the British League. This was a move that ensured that there would be team places for many more riders, albeit in a lower division, and that young riders would not be left to stagnate in the second halves. It would, and did, nurture the stars of the future, just as the Provincial League before it had. A rule that was introduced for the first time in the British League was that any rider who broke the tapes would be excluded from that race.

Cradley's first match was at Brandon in a League fixture against Coventry Bees, and the Heathens got hammered. This was their traditional start of the season, so no one got too excited about the result, although it should be pointed out that Bob Andrews had not yet arrived from New Zealand. When Bob did arrive a few days later, he appeared in the Crossroads Trophy at Monmore Green. The Heathens gremlin was hungry after coming out of hibernation and struck immediately, claiming Andrews at Wolverhampton with a broken collarbone, and so the first Heathen was out, even before he had made his debut!

19th MEETING   10th AUGUST 1968
7.30 p.m.

CRADLEY HEATH
SPEEDWAY

BRITISH SPEEDWAY LEAGUE

CRADLEY HEATH

v

WIMBLEDON

OFFICIAL PROGRAMME — PRICE ONE SHILLING

1968 programme cover.

Cradley bought in the ever-faithful Alan Totney to cover Andrews in the return against the Bees, but the Heathens failed in their home debut by 4 points, Trigg dropping his only point to Ron Mountford. A visit to Exeter saw Cradley score only 16 points, although the match featured some vintage Julian. In his first outing, he was excluded for putting Tommy Sweetman into the safety fence, and in his next, he shoved team-mate Roy Trigg, almost causing him to fall. Just to get things straight right from the 'off', Triggy rode round to Chris at the end of the race and thumped him!

Bobby Andrews made his comeback at Newport and scored 7 points as Cradley scraped 31 points in all. The following night at Dudley Wood, he scored only 6 points against Exeter and was obviously still wary, but Brown, Bergqvist and Trigg all scored well to win the match for the Heathens. With the team settling down, it was about time the gremlin struck again, and right on cue, he broke two of Tommy Bergqvist's ribs and Tommy went home to Sweden to recuperate. Even so, Cradley went to Glasgow with six men and came away with a draw – Trigg, Andrews and Julian being the heroes.

Peter Wrathall was brought in once again, and capitalised on Bergqvist's misfortune by scoring 5 points at Dudley Wood against Poole. Ken Wakefield responded to the competition and put on his best display for the Heathens to date, scoring 7 points. With Coombes and Brown in good form, Cradley won comfortably. The Heathens then moved on to Roy Trigg's old hunting ground and took on Oxford at Cowley. Roy thundered to a brilliant 15-point maximum, and a fine all-round performance saw Cradley win by a clear 17 points.

The Heathens were riding better than ever as a team, and notched up their fifth consecutive victory at Dudley Wood against Sheffield before losing by just 1 point at Custom House, when they almost ended West Ham's twelve-month unbeaten home run. The answer was Trigg and Andrews. They had quickly forged Cradley into a solid team, and the management had finally signed a couple of riders that were doing what they had bought been brought in to do.

Cradley fans were forced to swallow their pride in mid-May, as Wolverhampton's super Swede Hasse Holmqvist took the Alan Hunt Trophy from Nigel

Lars Jansson. (Speedway Star)

1968 team line-up. Grahame Coombes, Peter Wrathall, Chris Julian, Ivor Brown (on machine), Tommy Bergqvist, Ken Wakefield, Roy Trigg, Bob Andrews. (Speedway Star)

Boocock and Colin Goody. Bob Andrews was the top Heathen, with 10 points and fourth place. Bergqvist returned to ride at Coatbridge, and when Cradley lost 51-27, one wondered if the bubble had burst. The Heathens responded by drawing away at Poole and Kings Lynn, thus moving up to sixth place in the British League. Although it was usually Trigg who scored double figures, all of the riders were chipping in with points and it was showing in the results.

Roy Moreton was once again team manager, Ted Flanaghan being tied up with duties as stadium manager, but Roy was unprepared for what happened in Cradley's next match at Dudley Wood against Newcastle. A 15-point Mauger maximum led the Diamonds to a 2-point win, and Flanaghan was unhappy with the Cradley team manager's tactical moves, or rather the lack of them, and Moreton was dismissed.

The Heathens travelled to Sheffield and got knocked out of the Knockout Cup and then lost away matches at Hackney and Belle Vue. The gremlin hit Ivor Brown in the second half at the Manchester track and he damaged his shoulder, putting him out of action for a month. Ken Wakefield moved up into the main body of the team, and Peter Wrathall was again recalled, but Cradley missed Brown's presence, and although they were still winning at home, they were now losing all their away matches and began to slide down the League table.

In a match at Newcastle, towards the end of June, gremlin favourite Tommy Bergqvist fell and broke four bones in his foot. It was the end of the season for Tommy and he returned to Sweden. He was never to appear again for The Heathens. Cradley quickly replaced Tommy with another Swede – Lars Jansson, younger brother of the highly accomplished Bengt, who rode at Hackney. Lars had found himself surplus to requirements at Glasgow in his first year in the British League, and was only too happy to throw in his lot with the Heathens. Twenty-four-year-old Lars was very much a stereo-typical Swede – blond hair, blue eyes and devastatingly handsome, with a 5ft 11in frame (generally, riders used to be much bigger in those days). He became very popular very quickly, especially with the female supporters.

His arrival coincided with a great patch of form by Graham Coombes, which helped Cradley win their next five matches – matches at home and the last one away at Swindon, where Ken Wakefield broke his collarbone. Lars settled down quickly. He scored 6 points in his debut, and continued to score well in subsequent matches. Meanwhile skipper Ivor Brown had returned, but he was riding under the handicap of severe pain and was only managing to score 4 or 5 points a match. But the way the rest of the lads were scoring took the pressure off Brownie and, at the beginning of August, Cradley were sitting pretty in fifth place in the League.

The Heathens were pulled up sharply when Leicester visited Dudley Wood in a Midland Cup match. The Lions boasted perhaps the finest heat-leader trio in the country in Ray Wilson, Anders Michanek and John Boulger, and with ex-Heathens Johnny Hart and George Major in the line-up, they beat Cradley by 4 points. Leicester were to prove a 'bogey' team for the Heathens and it was to be some time before Cradley finally beat their Midland rivals.

Against Wimbledon in the next home match, Wrathall, who was back in the team to replace the injured Wakefield, fell and sustained leg injuries, joining Wakey on the

Ken Wakefield in action. (Speedway Star)

Graham Coombes.

sidelines. For a special challenge match at Dudley Wood, Cradley recalled Alan Totney to ride against the Czech touring team Prague. Alan did well to score 2 points in as many outings, but the star of the show was Lars Jansson, who rode to his first maximum – on a borrowed bike to boot! It was one-way traffic as the Heathens won the encounter by a clear 33 points.

Towards the end of August, Cradley won the Dudley/Wolves Trophy from holders Wolverhampton. Both legs were thrilling affairs, and although Holmqvist rode brilliantly in both, Andrews was equally impressive for Cradley. The Heathens won their home leg by 16 points and lost by only 7 points at Monmore Green with a very solid team performance.

Cradley's next home match was on the last day of August, when they unmercifully thrashed Oxford in an incident-packed match. Cheetahs' Ronnie Genz was rushed to hospital with a fractured skull and Jansson and Brown were the Heathens' hospital visitors, although Lars returned before the end of the meeting minus the end of one of his fingers. The already bruised and battered Brown was found to have broken his ankle and heat ten was the last race he was to ride for Cradley. It was the end of an era. The haunting days were over for the White Ghost of Dudley Wood.

Ivor Brown had been Cradley's greatest servant to date. In eight consecutive seasons he had given his all, and much more. The man who had once reigned supreme had, due to a never-ending series of injuries, been beaten into submission. The battle-weary warrior would fight no more; the pain had become too much. Cradley would never forget Ivor Brown, nor the debt that they owed him for his leadership through some very dark days.

The Heathens lost their next three matches; two at home to Halifax and Leicester. They also lost Wrathall for the rest of the season with a shoulder injury. His place was taken by juniors Archie Wilkinson and local lad Chris Hawkins.

Cradley won the rest of their home meetings and lost their away fixtures. Trigg, Julian and Andrews all scored well, and Wakefield came back better than ever, but the supporters were generally disappointed with the Heathens' fourteenth place out of nineteen in the League. True, it had been their best performance ever, but earlier in the season they had been up there challenging for the leadership. But let's not forget, not only did they have the other eighteen teams to contend with, there was the Cradley gremlin also, and he had a very lively year. Coventry won the British League and, ironically, in the year that saw the last of Brown, Ivan Mauger won his first World Championship. Roy Trigg topped the Heathens averages, followed by Andrews, Coombes, Julian, Jansson, Brown and Wakefield.

16

CRADLEY'S SUPER SWEDE
1969

The year 1969 saw Cradley sign their first world-class rider. True, Andrews HAD been there, Trigg was almost there, but Bernt Persson WAS there. He had been in the previous two World finals, and, at twenty-three years old, he looked as though he would be in many more. Bernie had made his debut in the British League with Edinburgh in 1965 and had moved with the rest of the team to Coatbridge, where he had blossomed into a heat-leader and Swedish international. It had been a rapid rise to the top for Persson, but then he was typical of so many of the Swedes, determined, detached, focused, and on occasions, quite ruthless – a legacy of Fundin in fact. The Coatbridge management were shocked to hear of Bernie's winter move, but the Heathens' fans immediately took him into their hearts.

Another winter acquisition for Cradley was the young Australian Chris Bass from Exeter, called in to replace Chris Julian who had moved on to Newport. Lars Jansson had decided to stay in Sweden, and Ivor Brown stayed true to his retirement plan and took over as co-promoter alongside ex-Heathen Vic White at Second Division Long Eaton. Alongside the two newcomers would be the new skipper Roy Trigg, Andrews, Coombes and Wakefield. As usual, the reserve spot turned into a bit of a 'bun fight', but by the start of the season it was Peter Wrathall who was given the green light. Russell Bragg was to act as team manager on Tuesdays and Fridays as Flanaghan would be tied up at the stadium with greyhound racing. Dare one say it – the Heathens appeared to have a strong line-up for 1969.

They began the season at Monmore Green on 4 April, and what a sweet opening to the year it was, thrashing Wolves on their own track 46-32. Trigg scored a maximum, and was well backed by Andrews (10), Persson (9), Bass (8), Coombes (3) and reserves Wakefield and Wrathall (2 points each). Holmqvist had not returned to England, and the Wolverhampton top-dog was now Norman Hunter. Although he battled gamely, he could not save his team from a 6-point defeat in the return at Cradley the following night. In the same match, Trigg dropped just a point and Persson, on his Dudley Wood debut, dropped only 2. Andrews and Bass were also impressive. Two League matches and two wins – a good start.

The Heathens' next engagement at Newport was controversial to say the least. The Heathens went into heat twelve represented by Trigg and Andrews, just 2 points down. Wasps' John Erskine broke the tapes and was excluded. His replacement was announced as Alby Golden, but Alby had already taken his allotted five rides. While

2nd MEETING   12th APRIL 1969

7.30 p.m.

CRADLEY HEATH
SPEEDWAY

CHRIS BASS   BERNT PERSSON

BRITISH SPEEDWAY LEAGUE

CRADLEY HEATH

v

NEWCASTLE

OFFICIAL PROGRAMME — PRICE ONE SHILLING

1969 programme cover.

1969 team line-up. From left to right: Ted Flanaghan (manager), Chris Bass (kneeling), Ken Wakefield, Grahame Coombes, Roy Trigg (on machine), Bob Andrews, Peter Wrathall, Bernt Persson (kneeling), Russ Bragg (team manager). (Speedway Star)

Cradley were protesting, Trigg and Andrews were excluded for exceeding the two-minute time limit, and Golden and partner Bob Hughes coasted round for a 5-0 heat win. The Cradley supporters rioted at the referee's box, and police and stadium security were called to restore order.

The final race, when it finally got underway, was won by Persson, but Wakefield trailed in last, making the score 42-35 in Newport's favour. The scratch races followed in due course, and at their commencement, the referee announced that heat twelve was null and void, so the Wasps had won the match 37-35! All of this had taken place as the supporters' club coaches were on their way home, and they were unaware of the correct score. Russell Bragg must have wished that he were at the dog track and that Flanaghan was at Somerton Park, but he stuck in an appeal and managed to get the result scrapped. It was decreed that the match was to be re-run at a later date.

Cradley won their next two home matches and lost at Coventry by only 4 points. Persson, Trigg and Andrews all scored well, but Coombes was struggling and had been excluded no less than three times in the first two meetings for breaking the tapes. Peter Wrathall had done as much as anyone could have expected of him, anyone apart from Ted Flanaghan that is, and in the middle of April he was replaced by Geoff Penniket. However, Geoff never settled down and he left to try his luck in the Second Division after a handful of matches. Wrathall, understandably miffed, had already dropped down and joined Long Eaton in a bid to get regular outings, so Cradley were forced to bring in Chris Hawkins. Chris was a game lad, but had only just begun riding and he was at the wrong stage of his career to be thrust into the strongest League in the world. He found the odd point very difficult to come by, leaving the Heathens' tail end weak.

The next two matches saw Cradley without Persson, who was fulfilling his Swedish obligations, and the Heathens were thrashed at Wimbledon, only just managing to beat the Dons at Dudley Wood a couple of nights later. Trigg hit top form and took great delight in beating his hero, the legendary Ronnie Moore, who had made his comeback to Britain that very year. Roy was the only rider to finish ahead of Moore at Plough Lane, and he did it twice at Cradley Heath, equalling the track record into the bargain.

Upon Bernie's return, the Heathens, thanks to some gritty performances by Bass and Wakefield, took on the look of a team the might have challenged for honours in 1969. Persson made his comeback in impressive style, lowering the track record to 68.2 seconds in his first ride and scoring a maximum against vanquished Poole. Cradley's next match saw them beat Halifax for the first time ever at Dudley Wood, and it was also the first time that Dukes' Dave Younghusband had dropped a point in the British League to a Cradley rider, Andrews and Trigg obliging. In the same match, just two nights after Persson had been declared track-record holder, he was deposed as Eric Boocock became the fastest man ever around Dudley Wood, doing four laps in 67.0 seconds.

During May, the Heathens began to dominate on their home track. Trigg won the World Championship qualifying round and Persson won the Midland Riders' qualifying round.

The Swede followed this by winning the Alan Hunt Trophy from Ivan Mauger and Bobby Andrews. On his way to the trophy, Bernie had become the first man to beat the incredible Ivan Mauger in 1969!

Persson had really settled down and was showing the best form of his career to date, as was Roy Trigg. Andrews was showing his best form since joining the Heathens, and Kenny Wakefield was beginning to beat some big-name riders. Lanky Ken had developed one of the most unique styles of riding. He sat bolt upright on his bike, and as he threw

Roy Trigg. (Speedway Star)

Chris Bass. (Speedway Star)

it into the corners, his long left leg would jut out at a right angle to his machine, making it virtually impossible to overtake him on the inside. Ken could hardly have been called 'poetry in motion', but his style was proving to be effective and he was picking up some good scores.

Graham Coombes, on the other hand, was having a poor season. As early as June, he announced that, at twenty-nine, he felt that he should be putting down roots, and at the end of the season he would be returning to New Zealand for good. Ted Flanaghan became Cradley's first injury victim when he fell in the stadium in May and cracked a couple of ribs. Impressive Chris Bass broke his collarbone towards the end of the month, but continued to ride, although it understandably affected his form. However, the Heathens did have three good heat-leaders for the first time ever and, with all of the team chipping in, they found themselves in third place in the British League.

Cradley entered the Midland Cup competition with a draw at Oxford, and after beating the Cheetahs in the re-run at Dudley Wood, they progressed into the next round of the Knockout Cup by beating Glasgow at Cradley Heath. Hackney proved to be too good for the visiting Heathens, and a Barry Briggs maximum helped to scupper them at Swindon.

At the end of June, Dudley Wood played host to its first full international, Great Britain *v.* Sweden. Unfortunately, it was not the Cradley boys who were to be the stars of the night, as Trigg scored only 5 points and Andrews 2 points for Great Britain, and Bernie fared a little better, scoring 8 points for Sweden. It was left to the likes of Nigel Boocock, Ray Wilson and Barry Briggs to lead Britain to an 18-point victory.

Poor old Chris Hawkins was having the life hammered out of him at reserve and was an obvious candidate for the Second Division where he could rebuild his shattered confidence. He was allowed the move, and Flanaghan made a very astute signing in young Mike Gardner. The nineteen-year-old Londoner had been putting on some good displays for Second Division Rayleigh, and Mike made his debut at Dudley Wood at the end of June. He settled in immediately, scoring 3 points in each of his first three matches. In fact, just two weeks after his arrival, the Heathens drew at Glasgow and Mike scored 9 points, a score that was bettered only by Trigg on the Cradley side. The Heathens were looking a match for any team in the League, Roy Trigg had progressed to the British final, and everything in the Cradley camp looked rosy. The gremlin was on a vacation that everyone hoped was a permanent one, and it appeared as if the bad old days were well and truly behind the Heathens.

In the middle of July, Cradley played host to Belle Vue, who were looking to win the League Championship themselves. They had acquired World Champion Ivan Mauger in the winter, and he was currently boasting an average of over 11.5 points. The Heathens had already been to Belle Vue in May, and having lost by only 2 points must have fancied their chances at Dudley Wood, but it was not to be. They were without Coombes, who had hurt his ankle at Glasgow the previous night, and therefore Hawkins was recalled.

Belle Vue had shown other teams the way with their forward thinking. When the Second Division was formed, the Aces had entered their own team, the Belle Vue Colts, and it spawned such stars as Eric Broadbelt and Chris Pusey. As the youngsters progressed, they would be given first-team outings to broaden their experience. Cradley lost their unbeaten record by 4 points, and the match-winner for Belle Vue was one of the Colts – Eric Broadbelt, who scored a magnificent 9 points. Mauger was unbeaten by an opponent and unselfishly 'shepherded' Broadbelt round for a 5-1 against Bobby Andrews. The Heathens were given a lesson in team-riding and dropped down a couple of places in the League table.

Meanwhile, Roy Trigg's World Championship campaign came to an abrupt halt as he finished last in the British final. He picked himself up, however, and led Cradley to victory in home matches for the rest of the month. One such match was against Swindon in the Knockout Cup, and although the Robins couldn't pull it off, Barry Briggs was superb and remained unbeaten all night, as well as successfully defending the Silver Sash against top-scoring Chris Bass.

The Heathens lost their next two away fixtures – at Oxford and Kings Lynn – and dropped to seventh place in the League table. However, at Oxford the Cheetahs had illegally used Colin Pratt as a guest and, when Cradley's subsequent protest was upheld, they were later awarded 2 points. The Heathens failed to get a rider into the World final again as Persson sustained an eye injury in the European final and failed to qualify. He was absent for Cradley's first match in August, which proved to be a memorable affair and one which is now part of Heathen folklore.

The match in question was at Dudley Wood and the visitors were bottom-of-the-table Hackney Hawks. Cradley elected to use rider replacement and beat the London outfit by 20 points, but not without some fun and games along the way. Hackney's lowly League position was possibly due to a problem that Cradley had experienced in previous years. Jack Biggs had come out of retirement to ride for the Hawks. Their line-up also featured veterans Les McGillivray and Jimmy Gooch. All good riders in their time, but too many veterans had put too much pressure on Hackney's top man, Colin Pratt.

However, they did have one young rising star in their ranks, the precocious Australian Garry Middleton. In a mere couple of years he had become one of the most controversial characters in the sport. On track he could be brilliant, but quite often he was completely ruthless. His off-track exploits ranged from 'rubbishing' much better riders than himself to punch-ups with his own team-mates. Quite a colourful character you will agree. Anyway, on this particular night, Garry was on form. He had an early match tussle with Bob Andrews that caused a bit of a furore, but things really reached boiling point in heat twelve when he lined up alongside fellow Hawk Gooch, and Cradley's Mike Gardner and Grahame Coombes.

The Heathens pair made the gate, but Middleton bored under both of them and Gardner ended up in the fence. The race was stopped, and as the Aussie made his way back to the pits, Coombes caught up with him and gave him a thump. Riders and officials alike were running from the pits to part the riders and by this time Gardner, who had recovered, had run across the centre green, removed his crash helmet, and had clouted Middleton across the head with it. Meanwhile, Mike's father had also run out of the pits and 'put the boot in'.

Order was eventually restored and the race was re-run without the excluded Middleton, but back in the pits, trouble once again broke out. It is rumoured that the irate Hawk drew a firearm and threatened his aggressors. Sense finally prevailed, due largely to Hackney captain Colin Pratt who gave his rider a dressing down in no uncertain terms. The Cradley fans were livid and began to gather at the pit entrance to await Middleton. Hackney manager Len Silver read the situation and drove his car down into the pits, but when he drove back out, the awaiting Cradley mob 'smelt a rat' and gathered around the vehicle. Suddenly, from under a blanket on the back seat, Garry Middleton's head popped out and all hell broke loose. The police were called and Silver's car was given a police escort from the stadium.

Cradley used rider replacement for Bernie in the next two matches, losing away and then winning at home. For the next two matches they brought in junior rider Mick Holmes, but he failed to score as the Heathens first beat Oxford and then lost to Coventry at home by 4 points in the first leg of the Midland Cup semi-final.

For the first leg of the Dudley/Wolves Trophy at Monmore, Cradley called in Leicester's Johnny Boulger and Malcolm Brown as they were three men short. Persson was not due back until the following day, Coombes had an ankle injury, and Bob Andrews was riding for New Zealand in a Test match against England. Erol Brook, who had made a comeback in the second halves at Cradley, found himself in the Heathens line-up for that first leg, but he had a pointless match. Cradley lost by just 4 points, and in the return leg the following night (this time with a full team), they won by 6 points to retain the trophy. Roy Trigg was unbeaten in both matches, and in the second leg at Dudley Wood, Mick Handley, who had developed into one of the top riders in the Second Division with Crayford, top-scored for the Wolves with 11 points.

The Heathens began September with a hammering at Halifax, and two nights later received the same treatment at Brandon, as Coventry knocked them out of the Midland Cup competition. Gardner rode with his hand in plaster, and Coombes was riding with an aggravated ankle injury, both as a result of the match at Halifax. The Cradley fans

Bernt Persson.

couldn't complain though – at this stage of the season they were more used to seeing most of their riders in hospital rather than on the track!

The Heathens' next match was against bogey team Leicester at Dudley Wood, and although Cradley failed to beat the Lions, they did hold them to a draw for the first time ever, thanks to a faultless Trigg maximum. The Heathens continued through

133

September, winning at home and losing away, but failing to pick up the odd point at the away tracks was costing them, and they found themselves stuck in seventh place in the League. Cradley did, however, have a favourable draw in the Knockout Cup semi-final with a home tie against Wimbledon. Bob Andrews had an off night, scoring only 2 points, and although Persson and Trigg both scored double figures, Wakefield was their only support, and the Heathens lost by 6 points and were out of the Knockout Cup.

If this was the low point of Bob's season, then it had quickly followed the high point of his whole career, for two days earlier he had lifted the World Pairs Championship with Ivan Mauger in Stockholm. It was a shock for Andrews to find himself in the event – first Barry Briggs withdrew from the New Zealand pairing after legal problems, and then, at the last minute, his replacement, Ronnie Moore, pulled out with an injured foot, leaving an opening for Bob.

Cradley's last three League fixtures were all away matches – at West Ham, Newcastle and Coatbridge – and, true to form, they lost them all. But they had still done enough to finish seventh in the League – their best ever season by far. Roy Trigg topped the Heathens' averages with 9.27 points and represented Cradley in the British League Riders' final where he finished in sixth place. Persson followed closely with 9.11 points.

There had been a definite change in the Heathens' fortunes in 1969. Apart from having three good heat-leaders, the answer was the lack of injuries to riders. Trigg missed only one meeting, when his car broke down en route to Newcastle; Andrews, Bass and Coombes also missed only one match each; and even Bernie, with his Swedish commitments and injured eye, only missed seven. Ken Wakefield was an ever-present.

The arrival of Persson had transformed the Heathens into a serious outfit. Flanaghan had shown that he was willing to build on that when he signed Mike Gardner to strengthen the bottom end. Mike had done what he had been brought in to do and gained a great following as a result. Chris Bass had also become a great favourite through his determined riding. Even with Ivan Mauger, Belle Vue failed to win the League Championship – that honour went to Poole. But the phenomenal Mauger had his own successes, successfully defending his World Championship and averaging an unbelievable 11.74 points. As the curtain was lowered on another season at Dudley Wood, the fans were taking interest in a young man who was putting it about a bit in the second halves at Cradley – Alan Hunt's son, Andy. Now if he could only turn out like his old man …

17
CUT OFF IN HIS PRIME
1970

The year 1970 found the sport of speedway thriving in Great Britain. There were thirty-six tracks operating on a weekly basis in both First and Second Divisions. The First Division looked as though it would start the new term with only eighteen teams when Coatbridge closed down, but as the new season approached, it was announced that Wembley Lions would roar again, and this time they would be led by the legendary Ove Fundin. It was an exciting time for speedway – Fundin was back, Ronnie Moore was back, Briggo was still in there with them, and of course, Ivan Mauger was about to begin his bid to become the only rider ever to win the World Championship three years in a row.

Ted Flanaghan had not been idle in the winter and, keen to keep up the momentum of the previous year, he had endeavoured to strengthen the team even further. On paper, he had achieved his objective. There were basically two new signings. The first one seemed a little questionable – Jimmy Squibb. Jimmy was no stranger to Dudley Wood, having been one of Ivor Brown's most formidable opponents back in the old Provincial League days. He had even ridden at Cradley in the late 1940s and early 1950s – so at least he knew his way there! But Squibby arrived at Dudley Wood at the grand old age of fifty. Having said that, he also arrived with an average of 7.31 points, and as he was replacing Graham Coombes, who had left with a 4.9 point average, it looked to be a good deal.

It must be said that Exeter were reluctant to let old Jimbo go; after all, he had always been good for 6 or 7 points a match and had never missed a match since the formation of the British League. It could be said that Jimmy Squibb was Mr Consistency personified. However, Jimmy's haulage business was suffering and he needed to join a Saturday track – so Jim became a Heathen. The next one was a 'biggie', a move that made Cradley look like potential League Champions. Hackney had agreed a straight swap – Bobby Andrews for Colin Pratt. The difference in their 1969 averages was negligible, but anyone who knew their speedway knew that Colin's 1969 average belied his true ability. He had simply had a disastrous '69 season by his own high standards.

Pratty was one of the success stories of the old Provincial League, where he rose to prominence with Stoke before moving to Hackney and leading them into the British League. He had finished third in the 1966 British final, and the following year saw him go all the way to the World Championship final as well as representing Great Britain in the World Team Cup final. He had ridden for Great Britain and England all over the world and had been London Riders' Champion in 1967 and 1968. Colin had contemplated retirement at the end of 1968, but had decided to sign with Hackney as their skipper for the 1969 season. It was not a happy one for Pratt and this was reflected in his riding. There was talk of unrest in the Hawks' nest, and Colin was known to have had a disagreement with manager Len Silver. He bided his time and come March 1970, he was a Heathen and Andrews was a Hawk.

It was a brave move by the Cradley management in some ways, because Bobby Andrews had always been very popular with Cradley riders and supporters alike, but Flanaghan was hungry for success and was not about to let his heart rule his head. Dudley Wood welcomed back Persson, Bass, Gardner, Wakefield and Roy Trigg, who had spent another winter riding in Australia and New Zealand. This year, Roy had bought a young Australian back with him to try his luck in the second halves – Malcolm Carmichael.

Bad weather caused Cradley's practice to be cancelled and they began the season at Wolverhampton with a challenge match at the end of March. Colin Pratt was on new machinery, and not having had the chance to sort it out at practice, he struggled in his debut and scored only 3 points, as did Chris Bass who was riding with an injury that he had sustained in Australia. Bernie Persson top-scored with 12 points as the Heathens lost by 8 points, but the star of the show was undoubtedly Wolves' winter signing, Ole Olsen, who scored a blistering maximum on his debut. Mauger had indeed taught him well.

The planned return match the following night at Dudley Wood was cancelled due to rain and frost, and on the following Saturday, the Heathens were away at Belle Vue, where they were methodically taken apart by the strong Manchester outfit. Trigg unsuccessfully challenged the unbeaten Ivan Mauger for the Golden Helmet (as the Silver Sash had now become) and, all in all, it was a very uninspired Cradley performance.

The Heathens at last made their home debut on Monday 6 April against Halifax. The winter had seen some alterations carried out to the Dudley Wood circuit, with a new drainage system and higher banking added. Whether or not this threw the Heathens is pure conjecture, but they lost by 3 points. Persson top-scored with 13 points and Trigg scored 10 points. Colin Pratt was known as a notoriously slow starter to the season, but he was sorting things out and at least scored an encouraging 6 points, but Squibb and Bass were right out of sorts.

Two nights later Cradley lost at Poole – four defeats from four matches, three of them in the League. It was hardly the best start for the potential League Champions. The fans were frustrated and some pointed the finger at Pratt. This seemed harsh because, whilst he was improving in every match, Gardener, Bass, Squibb and, to a lesser extent, Wakefield were showing nothing like the form that had been expected from them. Colin was a professional, however. He kept his head down and got on with it, and in the Heathens' next home match he silenced his critics with three heat wins and 10 points, as Cradley easily beat Glasgow to notch their first win of the season.

The Heathens narrowly lost by 2 points at Newcastle, and although Triggy beat Olsen's replacement, the very talented Anders Michanek, it was the start of a patch of bad form for Roy that saw him score only 5, 4 and 3 points in the next three matches.

19th Meeting   25th July 1970

7.30 p.m.

CRADLEY HEATH
SPEEDWAY

JAN SIMENSEN

BRITISH SPEEDWAY LEAGUE

CRADLEY HEATH

v

HACKNEY

OFFICIAL PROGRAMME — PRICE ONE SHILLING

1970 programme cover.

1970 team line-up. From left to right: Chris Bass, Ted Flanaghan (manager), Bernt Persson, Jimmy Squibb, Ken Wakefield, Roy Trigg (on machine), Colin Pratt, Mike Gardner, Russ Bragg (team manager). (Speedway Post)

Cradley could not afford to carry a heat-leader in their next home match against the mighty Belle Vue and subsequently they lost, but the match is also a part of Heathen folklore. It was the match that made Colin Pratt the new 'Golden Boy' at Dudley Wood. Up until that match, Ivan Mauger had not been beaten so far that year in the British League, and after two wins at Cradley, it looked unlikely that he would be beaten on that particular night, but Pratty had other plans. He was to meet Ivan in heats eleven and thirteen.

In heat eleven, Mauger made one of his super starts, but Colin would not be denied and stayed with the World Champion all the way until he pressured the Kiwi into making that one mistake. It was all that Pratt needed as he shot through on the inside to take the win. The stadium was in uproar, but Colin hadn't finished yet. In the last race of the match, he actually out-gated Mauger, and despite a spirited challenge from the Belle Vue Ace, Pratt once again crossed the line in first place. It was a pity that Colin could not have made it a hat-trick and relieved Mauger of the Golden Helmet in their Match Race, but he must have been more than happy to have done what no man had done since God knows when – beat Mauger twice in the same match.

In Cradley's next match at Wolverhampton, Pratt again top-scored with 9 points, but when Persson retired with 'flu after two outings, Colin received no backing whatsoever and the Heathens lost by 26 points. Pratt was in full flight by now, and May saw him win the World Championship qualifier at Dudley Wood and also finish runner-up to Ole

Olsen in the Alan Hunt Trophy. Mauger and Briggs finished third and fourth, so that says something about the opposition he was up against. Trigg managed to pick himself back up for a couple of meetings, and Cradley even won an away match at Oxford, but they lost their next three League matches – two of them at home – and then got knocked out of the Knockout Cup at Wimbledon. It was the end of May, and the Heathens were at the bottom of the League.

Persson and Pratt were riding well, but Triggy was up and down like a yo-yo. It was a pleasant surprise when he finished in fourth place in the British semi-final at Sheffield, and an unpleasant surprise when Colin Pratt failed to qualify on the same night. It had to be said that it was the other four riders that were to blame for Cradley's present plight. True, any of them could pop up with an occasional good score, but the fact remained that in the last 4 matches, Bass, Gardner, Wakefield and Squibb had scored only 21 points between them! Skipper Roy Trigg gave the fans something to cheer about when he clinched third place in the British final behind Ivan Mauger and Ronnie Moore and was named Man of the Match. It was perhaps the high point of Roy's career,

Colin Pratt, Bernt Persson and Roy Trigg. (Speedway Star)

as he had a history of failing to give his best in 'the big meetings'. Bernie had also been 'doing the business' in Sweden and he had qualified for the Nordic final.

Russ Bragg, who was now team manager at all matches, was desperate and approached Arne Pander, the 'Great Dane' who had not ridden for some two years. Back in the early 1960s, Arne was recognized as being one of the top boys in the sport, but more than his fair share of injuries had forced him into retirement. He went through the motions, however, and put in a few appearances in the second halves, riding a track spare, but it soon became obvious that the Dane was not the answer. In fact, there was no answer. The year before, Flanaghan had recognized a problem at the bottom end of the team and had brought in Gardner and solved it, but this year, the problem was four riders and that was over half the team!

In Cradley's last match in May, they narrowly beat Newcastle at Dudley Wood and then lost the next four on the trot – two at home and two away. The Heathens' management were desperate and applied for permission to sign another rider. This was granted and, on Persson's recommendation, they signed his Swedish club-mate, Jan Simensen. The slender, lanky Swede arrived in time for Cradley's Midland Cup match at Monmore Green and replaced Wakefield in the reserve berth. The meeting started off brightly enough when Persson beat the almost invincible Ole Olsen, but the Heathens were forced to face the Wolves the following night at Dudley Wood, 6 points in arrears. It had been a useful debut for Simensen though, for despite bouncing off the safety fence three times in one race, he still managed to score 5 points.

Olsen began the return leg at Dudley Wood by lowering the track record to 66.4 seconds, much to the disgust of the Cradley fans. The rivalry between the two clubs was by now in full swing, and the Heathens' fans were giving Olsen the same kind of reception that the Wolves' fans had given Ivor Brown in the early 1960s. Same reason really – he was so very, very good. However, on the night, Trigg and Pratt both got the better of him, and the Heathens won the match by 8 points to move into the next round.

Chris Bass finally came to life and topped the Cradley scorechart with 12 points, but this was not the talking point of the match. In heat eleven, Olsen was beaten by Colin Pratt. Now, whether or not Ole thought that Colin was not worthy of beating him is a matter of conjecture, but he faced him again in the last race, with Roy Trigg thrown in for good measure. Trigg made the gate, and Olsen followed him out. As the race progressed, Ole turned around and noticed Pratt hot on his heels and waved him past! Colin naturally seized his opportunity and took up second place, only to be passed by Olsen who followed Trigg home. Ole's explanation for this was that he wanted to prove that he could beat Colin, and thought that he could also pass Triggy later on in the race. All very modest I'm sure, but the fact remains that Cradley only won on aggregate by 2 points, so his tactics must have raised some questions at management level.

Roy Trigg had suffered his fair share of problems so far in 1970 and felt that he could do without the added responsibility of being captain, so he asked to be relieved of the post. The rider's choice for the vacant position was Colin Pratt, and although Colin didn't relish the job, he accepted and made his debut as the new Heathens skipper toward the end of June at his old haunt, Hackney. What a debut it was too. He packed

Jimmy Squibb. (Speedway Star)

twice when in the lead, was excluded on two minutes by a split second in another outing, and finished the match with a nil return (Bobby Andrews scored 7). Needless to say, Cradley were not victorious on this particular occasion.

Cradley moved into July with three wins at Dudley Wood – against Newport, Coventry and Oxford. The main reason for this upturn in results was Simensen. True, he was still hitting the fence (and the occasional lamp standard), but he was returning any thing between 6 and 9 points per match and it was making the difference. The Heathens could have been excused for thinking that they were on their way up, but their troubles had just begun – Colin Pratt had ridden his last match for Cradley.

Colin had been given permission to ride for a West Ham Select side in Holland, so after the Oxford match, he and young Malcolm Carmichael set off to join the party. After a successful match, they were making their way back through Belgium by van when they were involved in a bad road crash in Lokren on 14 July. Colin was badly injured with a broken neck and cracked kneecap, and he was one of the lucky ones. Team manager Phil Bishop and riders Martyn Piddock, Garry Everett, Pete Bradshaw and Malcolm Carmichael were all killed on speedway's blackest day. At thirty-one, Colin Pratt's speedway career was over. Cradley had been robbed of another Golden Boy and England had been robbed of an international. But it was not the last that Cradley would see of Colin Pratt.

When the shock waves had died down at Dudley Wood, the rest of the team went about their business, but the season was virtually over for the Heathens. All that they could do was to try to salvage some pride from the rest of the year, which to a certain extent they did. They won all of their home matches in August, and had only one hiccup when they lost their Cradley leg of the Dudley/Wolves Trophy by 6 points. Trigg scored a scorching 17 points and beat Olsen twice. Jan Simensen was improving all the time, and he won the Oxford qualifying round of the Midland Riders' Championship, but on the downside, Trigg and Persson both made their exits from the World Championship competition.

The second leg of the Dudley/Wolves Trophy took place at Monmore Green at the beginning of September and was a torrid affair. Wolves were without Olsen, and Cradley trailed the home side by 4 points with just one race remaining. Trigg, Persson and

Simensen had all scored well and Gardner was having one of his better nights, and although the Trophy was lost, the match could still be drawn. In heat thirteen, Persson and Gardner made the gate on Mick Handley and Peter Vandenberg and the Heathens were in a position to share the match. On the last bend, Handley brought down Gardner, and although the Wolves rider was excluded, Gardner was awarded third place, which effectively cost Cradley the match. The crowd was in uproar, and certain members of the Cradley contingent jumped over the fence, onto the dog track and began to make their way to the pits to 'sort Handley out'. They had picked on the wrong one, however, and Mick, not the least bit intimidated, had left the pits, got onto the dog track and was walking to meet them head on, like a scene from *High Noon*. The police were called, there were scuffles in the pits and in the crowd, and the activities continued even during the presentations. There's nothing like these Dudley/Wolves Trophy meetings!

Meanwhile, the Heathens had recalled Ken Wakefield back to the fold, but Ken, probably upset at having been dropped in the first place, failed to appear for any of his programmed appearances. Glynn Chandler had made a comeback in the second halves at Dudley Wood, and he found himself making a couple of first-team appearances, as did Mick Holmes and Malcolm Shakespeare, but generally, Cradley rode the rest of the season with just six riders. Coventry beat them in the Midland Cup semi-final, but the Heathens were riding well and lost by only a handful of points at both Glasgow and Wembley before forcing a draw at Sheffield. They moved up a few places in the League, but it was far too late in the season to make an impact of any real kind.

At the end of September, Cradley played host to Wolverhampton in a League match, but by line-up time they found themselves with only five riders. Persson was away winning the World Team Cup with Sweden, so the Heathens had been given permission to use Garry Middleton, of all people, as a guest. They were forced to include both Chandler and Holmes, and both failed to score, as did Gardner, and Cradley lost a very bad-tempered affair by just a point. Both opponents and team-mates argued furiously in the pits and nearly came to blows. Some idiot sprayed Mick Handley's car with diesel, but the Cradley management took care of the bill.

For their last home match of 1970, the Heathens attempted once again to beat Leicester in a challenge match, but their efforts were in vain and the Lions remained unbeaten at Dudley Wood. Cradley at least went out on a high, winning their final League match at Newport, which put them in fifteenth place in the final League table. However, even sweeter than that, they won the final match of the season at Monmore Green – a challenge match against their old rivals, Wolverhampton. Belle Vue, led by the incredible Ivan Mauger, won the League by a clear 11 points.

Bernt Persson was top Heathen with an average of 9.29 points, almost a full point ahead of Roy Trigg. Simensen had been a success and had finished the season with a 7.5-point average, which was just below Colin Pratt. The way Colin was riding when he had his accident indicated that he would have improved on that no end, but it was not to be. The Cradley management were left with a hell of a lot to do in the winter months. It had been a very bleak season for the Cradley Heathens.

18
CRADLEY'S FIRST WORLD FINALIST 1971

Cradley adopted a 'bring 'em back alive' policy to form their 1971 squad as, unable to get new riders, they brought back the old ones. They had retained the services of Persson, Trigg and Squibb, and decided to build the team around these three stalwarts. Colin Pratt had never given up his fight to return to the saddle, and indeed, if he ever did, then he pledged his allegiance to the Heathens. But it would not be in 1971 – if ever. Gardner had gone, so had Wakefield, and Chris Bass has decided to stay in Australia.

So, they brought 'em back. Back came Bobby Andrews, after just one unsuccessful season at Hackney, and back came Johnny Hart from Leicester. Cradley were desperate to hold onto Jan Simensen, but the SRA vetoed the move and withdrew the Swede's work permit on the grounds that the Heathens could not use two foreign riders. There were many other clubs using more than two and Cradley appealed, but the SRA were unrelenting. So enter one Pete Jarman.

Thirty-six year old Pete was well known in the Midlands, having made a name for himself at Stoke alongside Colin Pratt. When Sun Street closed, he moved on to Wolverhampton and battled against the Heathens on many occasions. Jarman arrived at Dudley Wood via Oxford, with the reputation of being one of the best team-men in the business. As usual, the number seven spot was a bit of a lottery.

Andrews was not due in England until Easter, and Cradley began their campaign without him in a challenge match at Monmore Green. They gave a good account of themselves, losing by just 1 point, but Ole Olsen looked awesome as he effortlessly rode to a superb maximum, and Ivan Mauger must have been wondering if this was the year that the pupil would eclipse the master.

The following night at Dudley Wood, Cradley opened their League programme with a match against Wimbledon. The Heathens had to track two novices, and Andy Bearne and Richard Eslick both failed to score as Cradley lost their first home match by 4 points. Newly-married Roy Trigg scored a superb maximum and was the only Heathen to beat Ronnie Moore. Persson was right behind Triggy, scoring 10 points, and Squibby looked good, scoring 7. Jarman and Hart had yet to find their feet, but still managed to score 4 points each. It was hardly the start the Cradley wanted, but they were, after all, carrying two passengers.

The Heathens were forced to field the same team for the next two matches (before Andrews returned) and also had a nasty shock when Persson was stretchered off after Barry Thomas rammed him in the first heat at Hackney. Bernie returned to the meeting against medical advice, but couldn't prevent Cradley from losing heavily. He was still in pain the following Saturday, when the Heathens narrowly beat Exeter by 1 point at Dudley Wood, but for the next match, five nights later at Glasgow, Bob was back.

He hardly set the stadium alight on his debut, scoring only 3 points as Cradley mustered only 30 points between them, and his 5 points the following night in the return were not enough to prevent the Tigers from winning by 2 points at Dudley Wood. In all fairness, the Heathens would have been likely to take the points had it not been for an engine failure by Persson in the last heat, but they should not have let Glasgow get so close in the first place.

Bob was obviously going to take a few matches to settle in, but the problem was that Persson and Trigg were getting little support from Hart and Jarman. Upon Andrews' return, Bearne went and Eslick stayed, for a few meetings that is, and then Cradley gave Mick Holmes a chance.

The World Championship qualifying round at Dudley Wood saw Heathens in first and third places, Roy Trigg and Pete Jarman respectively, with Garry Middleton splitting the two.

Cradley saw out April by losing at Coventry and beating the Bees at home, and began May with a trip to Smallmead to take on the mighty Anders Michanek and his Reading Racers. The Heathens started off lively enough as Persson headed Michanek home in the first race. Andrews repeated the feat some races later, and going into heat eleven Cradley were on level terms. If Trigg had not suffered a sick motor all night, scoring only 4 points, the Heathens may have pulled it off, but they eventually lost by 6 points. Jarman and Hart got their act together and top-scored in Cradley's next match, a home win against Sheffield, but in the LP Transport Trophy a few nights later, the Heathens lost Pete with a broken ankle. Persson had to settle for second place in the event behind the devastating Ivan Mauger.

Jan Simensen had finally been granted a work permit, but it was to ride at Coventry. He guested for Cradley, who went to Kings Lynn minus Jarman, and also Trigg, who was away trying to conquer Poland with the rest of the Great Britain team. The Heathens had also brought in the ex-Wolverhampton Swede Bengt Andersson at reserve in an attempt to boost their flagging tail end. He scored 2, Simensen scored 8, Bernie scored 15; Cradley got beaten. After managing only a draw against Wembley at Dudley Wood, the Heathens beat Oxford away and at home to progress into the next round of the Midland Cup, but they were way down in the British League and looked like staying there.

As Cradley entered May, Persson was riding better than ever and scoring big points at every match. He had finished third in the Swedish rounds of the World Championship, and the Cradley fans were keeping their fingers crossed to have their first ever World finalist. Mauger was, of course, fantastically consistent, at all levels, but apart form him, Wolverhampton had 'The Man' – Olsen – and Cradley went to visit him

YOUR LUCKY NUMBER IS № 0632

19th MEETING
31st JULY, 1971
at 7.30 p.m.

Cradley Heath Speedway

JIMMY SQUIBB

K.O. CUP — 3rd ROUND

CRADLEY HEATH
versus
GLASGOW

OFFICIAL PROGRAMME - SEVEN NEW PENCE

1971 programme cover.

1971 team line-up. From left to right: Roy Trigg, Barry Duke, Bernt Persson, Bob Andrews, Jimmy Squibb, Pete Jarman, John Hart, Russ Bragg (manager). Inset: Mike Handley.

on 4 June. They lost by 8 points at Monmore and, apart from an engine failure, Ole was unbeaten and successfully defended his Golden Helmet against Persson. The following night at Dudley Wood, it looked as though the Heathens were finally going to beat their 'bogey' side, Leicester. Cradley were 2 points up going into the last race and when Trigg out-gated Ray Wilson, the writing was on the wall. However, Roy fell and Andrews followed Wilson home and the result was a draw. Poor old Triggy was having diabolical luck with his motors and had scored only 6 points total in 2 matches for Cradley since his return from Poland. His bad luck stayed with him throughout the British semi-final and he was out of the World Championship race.

After losing at home to Reading, the Heathens visited them for the seemingly impossible task of progressing to the next round of the Knockout Cup competition – and won! A blistering performance by Persson saw him take one complete second off Ole Olsen's track record, beating Michanek in heat one, and he stormed through the match unbeaten. With fine performances by Trigg, Andrews and Jimmy Squibb, the Heathens were through by a clear 2 points.

Andersson had failed to make an impact at reserve, so Cradley gave the job to ex-Swindon Robin, Barry Duke. Barry's arrival coincided with another slump in Roy Trigg's form, and the Heathens lost their next four matches. Roy scored a total of only 17 points in all four, but he managed to pick himself up in July. He began at Dudley Wood in the Midland Riders' Championship qualifying round, scoring 12 points, as did Bobby Andrews. Bernt Persson was just behind them on 11 points, but they all finished behind that man Olsen, who cruised to a 15-point maximum. Nine days later he again showed his liking for the Dudley Wood circuit, this time winning the Alan Hunt Trophy from Mauger and Briggs, with Trigg being top Heathen in fifth place. It was a classic meeting, with Olsen and Mauger being forced into a run-off for the trophy. Mauger, you will recall, was the one who had taken Ole under his wing at Newcastle when the Dane had arrived there in 1967. There was obviously something a little special about Olsen even in those days, but Ivan could never have expected him to be his main rival in such a short amount of time. If Olsen had learned riding techniques from Ivan, he had also learned gating tactics, and getting them up to the tapes together in those days was a starting marshall's nightmare!

July saw Bobby Andrews produce the best form of his Heathens career. His 15-point maximum at Wembley was breathtaking, and he only failed to score double figures once in the next six matches. But while he was 'doing the business', others were not and Cradley managed only two wins in June – but they were important wins. The first was a League match, but not just any old League match. It was a League match at Dudley Wood against Wolverhampton, and was a typically incident-packed Cradley/Wolves affair involving great racing, fists flying, and the police being called to the pits. Persson clashed with Gary Peterson, and Squibby exchanged a few blows with Jon Erskine, but Jon was man enough to apologise before the evening was over and everyone went home as friends. The other match was a 2-point win against Glasgow at Dudley Wood, which put the Heathens through to the Knockout Cup semi-final – against Wolverhampton! The Glasgow match saw the return of Pete Jarman, who impressed with a score of 8 points.

On a visit to Wimbledon, Persson, Andrews and Trigg all scored 10 points but the other four riders couldn't even score another 10 points between them! The result was a 2-point win for the Dons. Cradley had an inconsistent August due to team-mates playing 'musical chairs'. If Squibb scored, Hart didn't; if Hart scored, Jarman didn't, and so it went on. One really didn't know what to expect of Roy Trigg: one match he would be brilliant, the next abysmal. Predictably, the Heathens got knocked out of the Midland Cup at Coventry.

Ironically, Barry Duke had his best meeting for Cradley when they easily beat Halifax at Dudley Wood at the end of August. He scored 7 points, but a deal had already been made with West Ham that saw Barry go to Custom House in a straight swap for the unhappy Mick Handley. Barry's finest performance for the Heathens was his last.

Cradley's next match was the first leg of the Dudley/Wolves Trophy at Monmore Green. Wolves had objected to the Heathens using Handley and their objection was upheld. A number of Heathens supporters were removed from the stadium for protesting a little too vigorously. Cradley were forced to bring in Bengt Andersson, and although he had a pointless return, a good all-round performance saw the Heathens come away with a draw.

Mick got his chance the next night in the second leg at Dudley Wood and his 5 points helped Cradley to a 10-point win and the trophy to boot. Although he had been unbeaten at Monmore, Olsen had to concede just 1 point at Cradley Heath to Roy Trigg. Apart from beating the arch-enemy, the Heathens had something else to celebrate: Bernie Persson had made it through to the World Championship final and was to become Cradley's first ever representative at the meeting. The Knockout Cup semi-final

Pete Jarman.

against Wolves was an anti-climax, as Wolves were without Olsen. Cradley hammered them unmercifully 50-28 and found themselves in the final against Hackney.

On 10 September 1971 in Gothenburg, Sweden, the World final programme informed us that rider number twelve was Bernt Persson from Sweden and Cradley

Heath, and the Heathens supporters finally felt that they really were a part of the World final scene. Bernie by no means disgraced himself by finishing in seventh place with 9 points, but Cradley supporters had a bitter pill to swallow. Ole Olsen had done what he had been threatening to do all season and deposed Ivan Mauger as World Champion. Ivan had to be content with second place, as his pupil stormed to a 15-point maximum to take the title back to Monmore Green.

The Heathens were forced to ride the next couple of matches without Persson, who was still in Sweden. They won at Dudley Wood against Poole and lost at West Ham in two matches that saw Mick Handley hit top form. Against Poole, he was robbed of a maximum by Odd Fossengen and top-scored with 11 points. At West Ham, he was Cradley's top scorer with 9 points, but in the next match at Cradley, against eventual League Champions Belle Vue, disaster struck in his first outing when he fell and cracked his collarbone.

In the very next race, Squibb fell and broke a bone in his hand and, just to round off the night, Jarman retired from the meeting after a spill in heat six. It goes without saying that the Aces won the match by a proverbial mile, and while Mauger was his usual immaculate self, one couldn't but help notice his partner, one of the Belle Vue

Bob Andrews. (Speedway Star)

Mick Handley. (Speedway Star)

starlets – Peter Collins – who rode his heart out for his 2 points.

By the time Cradley faced Swindon two nights later, Jarman was back but the news on the other two was not so good. Squibb would be out for the rest of the season, the first British League matches that he had ever missed, and Handley would miss the next three matches. With Bengt Andersson and young Geoff Bouchard in the team, the Heathens failed to beat the Robins at Dudley Wood, and by the time they visited Poole, they had ex-Wolves rider Cyril Francis in the team. Cyril had a run of four matches, but failed to make an impression so late in the season.

Handley made his comeback, scoring 6 points against Oxford at Cowley on the last day of September. It was Cradley's last League match, and a 2-point defeat saw them finish bottom but one in the final League table. They had won only 8 League matches, and although they had had their fair share of injuries, they had been heavily punished for their inconsistency.

The Heathens' final home fixture of 1971 was the first leg of the Knockout Cup final against Hackney. The scorers were as follows: Persson (11), Andrews (9), Handley (7), Jarman (6), Hart (5), Trigg (3), and Francis (0). Cradley took just a 4-point lead to Hackney, which few suspected would be enough, especially as skipper Persson would be back in Sweden and unable to ride. It was a case of 'always the bridesmaid, never the bride', as guest Howard Cole was the only rider on the Cradley side to emerge with any credit. The Hawks thumped the Heathens 51-27 to win the cup by 20 points on aggregate.

It had been a miserable season for Cradley in which the highlights had been few and far between. Bernie Persson had ridden himself into Heathens history and had once again topped the Cradley averages with almost a clear point over Bob Andrews. Cradley supporters were left wondering how on earth they were going to face the Wolverhampton supporters now that they boasted the World Champion!

19

WORLD FINAL RUNNER-UP
1972

Cradley's 1972 season was all about Bernie Persson. He stood head and shoulders above anyone else in the team and proved himself to be of the highest calibre in world speedway. Russ Bragg still held the managerial reins, but Morris Jephcott was back as clerk of the course, and on the eve of the season, Morris launched a full-scale attack on the Rider Control Committee. Cradley had tried to sign ex-Wolves rider Dave Hemus for their 1972 campaign, but the move had been vetoed and the Heathens, with the same squad as the year before, had the lowest average in the League.

What Jephcott wanted to know was why League Champions Belle Vue were allowed a team average of 50.42 when Cradley's was as low as 44.25? His question fell on deaf ears. However, the management had taken note of Belle Vue's success with their youngsters, and 1972 saw the start of a training scheme for Cradley juniors that saw them with their own events in the second halves as well as regular Wednesday night practice matches.

The Heathens began with three home matches and won them all before their first away match at Monmore Green. Wolves had built their team around World Champion Ole Olsen and Norman Hunter, but Cradley seemed to have better all-round strength and lost only by 2 points. Persson, Trigg and Andrews were the Heathens' heat-leaders, Jarman and Squibb were the second strings, and Hart and Handley were the reserves.

The Heathens were unlucky not to beat Leicester in April when a mid-match retirement by Handley and a puncture by Hart cost Cradley the match at Dudley Wood. They did manage to hold the Lions to a draw, but Leicester remained unbeaten by the Heathens. Cradley won the rest of their home matches and lost all of their away ones in April.

Meanwhile, the junior riders were benefiting from their extra outings under the watchful eye of Jephcott, and Gerald Smitherman, Dave Perks, Dave Harvey and Ian Ross were all beginning to impress. Andy Hunt continued riding in the juniors, but one began to wonder if he would ever improve sufficiently to make it in the sport. All of the youngsters were given great support by a band of dedicated Cradley supporters who called themselves the action committee, The 'AC' had approached a number of local businessmen for sponsorship and they presented each junior with a new set of leathers. What started off as a commendable gesture turned into an incredibly messy business as the action committee and the supporters' club constantly bickered throughout the whole season.

As May arrived, Persson was going like a train and rattling off the maximums. At Dudley Wood, Cradley looked a good team, but on the away tracks, Jarman, Squibb and

CRADLEY HEATH SPEEDWAY
CRADLEY HEATH SPEEDWAY
CRADLEY HEATH SPEEDWAY
CRADLEY HEATH SPEEDWAY
CRADLEY HEATH SPEEDWAY
CRADLEY HEATH SPEEDWAY

18th MEETING
SATURDAY, 15th JULY, 1972
at 7.30 p.m.

Cradley Heath Speedway

CRADLEY HEATH SPEEDWAY
CRADLEY HEATH SPEEDWAY
CRADLEY HEATH SPEEDWAY
CRADLEY
CRADLEY
CRADLEY
CRADLEY
CRADLEY
CRADLEY
CRADLEY
CRADLEY
CRADLEY
CRADLEY
CRADLEY
CRADLEY
CRADLEY
CRADLEY
CRADLEY
CRADLEY
CRADLEY
CRADLEY
CRADLEY
CRADLEY
CRADLEY
CRADLEY
CRADLEY HEATH SPEEDWAY
CRADLEY HEATH SPEEDWAY
CRADLEY HEATH SPEEDWAY
CRADLEY HEATH SPEEDWAY
CRADLEY HEATH SPEEDWAY
CRADLEY HEATH SPEEDWAY
CRADLEY HEATH SPEEDWAY
CRADLEY HEATH SPEEDWAY

BOB ANDREWS

BRITISH LEAGUE CHAMPIONSHIP

CRADLEY HEATH
versus
KINGS LYNN

1972 programme cover.

1972 team line-up. From left to right: Roy Trigg, Mick Handley, John Hart, Jimmy Squibb, Bernt Persson (on machine), Russ Bragg (manager), Bobby Andrews, Ian Ross. (Speedway Star)

Hart struggled and the Heathens rarely scored 30 points. At Exeter without Bernie, who was on World Team Cup duty with Sweden, the Heathens received a right going over, and Roy Trigg had a nightmare evening. He blew his entire engine in his first race, got himself excluded in another, scored only 1 point all night, and when his car developed a fault, he was forced to drive most of the way back without lights! He did, however, fare a little better than Mick Handley, who got left behind due to a misunderstanding and had to hitch a lift back home!

Cradley lost their home record in May to Reading Racers. Persson scored another superb maximum, beating Anders Michanek in the process, but he received little support and the Heathens lost by 12 points. At the end of the twelfth heat, Cradley were losing 32-40 and as Morris Jephcott took over on the mike for the lucky programme draw, he had the crowd in stitches when he announced: 'We haven't lost this one yet!' Johnny Hart was heard telling Triggy and Andrews to go out and win the last heat 9-0! After the match, Pete Jarman had an enforced two-week lay-off because of nervous exhaustion. When Cradley visited Halifax, young Ian Ross made his debut in the side, scoring 4 points as the Heathens again failed to score 30 points away from home.

Handley had sustained concussion in his first outing at Halifax. It was typical of Mick's luck that when he was riding well, he suffered an injury. Two days before the Halifax match, he scored 11 points in the World Championship qualifying round at Dudley Wood – a meeting won with a vintage performance from Bob Andrews. Without Handley, Gerald Smitherman found himself alongside Ross when the Heathens played

Pete Jarman and Bernt Persson. (Speedway Star)

host to Coventry at the beginning of June. Although Cradley beat the Bees, Gerald failed to score. Ross, on the other hand, gave another encouraging performance, scoring 3 points – so encouraging that Bragg used him for the next four matches in place of the 'out of sorts' Jimmy Squibb.

The beginning of June saw Persson qualify for the Nordic final, with the Cradley fans willing him to go all the way again so that they could support him in their own country at Wembley. The Heathens arrived at Glasgow with their full team, Handley and Jarman having recovered, and came away with a point. However, they could only manage another draw with visiting Reading at Dudley Wood in the Knockout Cup and were booked in at Waterden Road for the replay. Squibb returned to the team at the end of the month, and Cradley beat Newport at Somerton Park. In the return at Dudley Wood the following night, the Heathens scored their biggest win ever, thrashing the Wasps 60-18 and moving up to sixth place in the League table.

Cradley entered July with a run of three defeats – at Hackney in the Knockout Cup, at Wimbledon, and at Dudley Wood against the newly promoted Ipswich. A return to form by Trigg saw the Heathens fare a little better as the month wore on, but when they faced Glasgow at Cradley, John Hart discovered prior to the meeting that his frame was cracked. He declined to use any replacement that was offered to him and insisted upon withdrawing from the meeting. Dave Perks was quickly drafted into the squad and made the best debut possible, when Andrews shepherded him round for a heat win in his first ever race for the Heathens. They were the only points that Dave scored all night, but Cradley won by 2 points and the fans were right behind Perks, who stayed in the team for the rest of the year. The reason for this was that Morris Jephcott had written a letter to John Hart stating that the management were of the opinion that his equipment was not up to scratch and that he should get it fixed and turn up for practice on Wednesday night. Hart's reply was unprintable. He never rode for the Heathens again.

The last away fixture in July was a Midland Cup match at Wolverhampton, and Cradley lost by a mere 2 points to a rather jaded Wolves and must have fancied their chances the following night in the second leg at Dudley Wood. The Heathens certainly made the right start as Persson beat Olsen in the first race, but the Dane made no further mistakes and led his team to a draw and a 2-point win on aggregate.

In August, the Alan Hunt Trophy was to be run on a handicap system for the first time. Depending on the rider's average, they were given points to start with. Bernie Persson, for example, had 1.81; Ole Olsen 0.95; Eric Boocock 2.25 etc. These points would be added to their final total, the winner being the rider with the most points at the end of the night. Ronnie Moore broke down on his way to the meeting and his place was taken by the first reserve Pete Jarman. Jarman had 8.88 'gift' points, and even though he fell in his first race, he scored 7 points in his last 4 rides, giving him a total of 15.8 points and the Alan Hunt Trophy! Poor old Terry Betts dropped only 2 points all night and scored 13 points, but his 'gift' points were only 1.98 and gave him a total of only 14.98 – less than Jarman. Needless to say, this method of scoring was not used again in subsequent events.

August was a disaster for Cradley as they failed to win a single match. Persson fought virtually a one-man battle, as Trigg's and Andrews' form took a nosedive and so did the Heathens' League position. But Persson had given the fans what they wanted – someone to cheer at the World Championship final at Wembley. He had made it all the way and was riding better than at any time in his career. Cradley got trounced at Belle Vue, but not before Bernie had beaten Mauger and Soren Sjosten in the first heat to stake his claim as arguably the best Swede in the British League at that time.

However, the final was not until the middle of September, and that gave the Heathens time to lose another four matches. In fact, the 2-point win that they had scored over Glasgow back in July was the last win that they were to have all season. Jimmy Squibb was again left out of the side to give Dave Harvey a run at reserve, but this time it was for good and Jim returned to

Roy Trigg in action.
(Speedway Star)

Bob Andrews. (Speedway Post)

Exeter on loan. On 16 September, a new World Champion was crowned. Ivan Mauger won his fourth world title, but not before he was forced into a run-off for the Championship with Bernie Persson. Even Cradley fans must have commiserated with Ole Olsen. He fell in his first race (which included Bernie) and was unbeaten in his other four rides to finish with 12 points and third place.

Persson was beaten in his first outing by fellow Swede Christer Lofqvist, and Mauger also dropped a point in his first to Barry Briggs. Bernt faced Briggs in his next outing, and Briggo crashed out of the final after clipping the Swede's back wheel. The crowd booed loudly, believing that it was Persson's fault, but Bernie was not the type to be put off by a hostile crowd. Like many of the top Swedes, he had ice in his veins. Mauger dropped a further point to Olsen, and arrived at the tapes to face Persson in heat nineteen with 10 points to his credit. Bernie had dropped no further points since his first outing, and led the field with 11 points.

To have any chance of regaining the title, Ivan knew what he had to do and he did it. A lightning gate by the Kiwi left Persson in his wake, but the Swede held on grimly to take second place and tie with Mauger on 13 points. Few had expected Bernt to do this well, but he had surpassed all expectations and at this moment was about to take place in a race that could make him World Champion. The run-off saw Ivan again make the gate, but Bernie stuck with him and for one glorious moment on the second bend of the last lap, it looked as though he would break through, but Mauger held him at bay and denied Cradley their first World Champion.

Bernie got a hero's reception when he returned to Dudley Wood, but there was little else to celebrate. The Heathens put up one poor performance after another, losing the Dudley/Wolves Trophy and dropping down the League to finish in sixteenth place, with only Oxford and Newport below them. It had been a dire season for Cradley. Apart from Persson, every rider was down on his average of the previous year. In contrast, the Swede had pushed his up to over that magic 10-point mark – 10.41 to be precise – which saw him finish in sixth position in the British League Riders' Averages. In short, Persson had joined the elite. He had ridden himself into the history books and had established himself as the greatest rider ever to wear Cradley colours.

20

AN ILL WIND OF CHANGE
1973

The year 1973 saw many changes at Cradley Heath. Russ Bragg relinquished his manager's post to take over the job at newly-built Chesterton in the National League (Second Division). His place was taken by the people's favourite, Harry Bastable. Harry was very enthusiastic about his new appointment and talked at length on how it was his intention to forge the new squad into a unit whose team spirit would be second to none. There would be a new race jacket, new riders and a new name. The team would now be known as Cradley United! Most supporters were unhappy with this idea but Bastable was quick to respond and went to great pains to explain that Cradley were still 'The Heathens' but now they were Cradley Heathens United. He reckoned that the name would represent a 'united front' to the rest of the British League and that perhaps a change of name would bring about a change of fortune, which Cradley could certainly use.

Harry retained only three of the 1972 squad. Bernt Persson returned as the kingpin of the side, and Pete Jarman and Dave Perks joined him. Cradley had recognised the potential that Perks had shown the year before when they were forced to use him in the team at a time when perhaps he was not ready for it. Perky had struggled, but the Heathens were willing to persevere, and with good reason because the twenty-one-year-old looked like one of the hottest prospects around. Dave had something else in his favour too; he was a local lad, hailing from just a few miles away in Halesowen. If there was anything the Cradley fans loved it was 'local boy makes good', and they were right behind Dave from day one.

Howard Cole was making a comeback at Dudley Wood after an absence of some six years. Since Howard had last appeared in Heathens colours, he had improved beyond recognition and had reached the World final in 1969. He had also been one of Kings Lynn's top riders following his departure from Cradley under a cloud of discontent. But now the hatchet was buried and Cole was prepared to give his all in an effort to win back his old fans at Dudley Wood. However, there was a problem – he was returning from injuries so severe that they had nearly finished his career and forced him to miss half of the 1972 season, so it could be said that Howard was a bit of a risk.

The next newcomer was London haulage contractor, Colin Goody. The thirty-eight-year-old was by no means a newcomer to speedway, having been a rider of some repute in the old National League back in the 1960s. Although Colin had never quite made the top flight, he could still beat anyone on his day and came to Cradley from Oxford. New

1973 programme cover.

Zealand international Bruce Cribb was the next of the new boys. He had been transferred from Exeter in the close season and arrived at Dudley Wood with a 9-point average, so the twenty-six-year-old New Zealand Champion was reckoned to be a good replacement for Trigg or Andrews. And last, but not least, a completely unknown quantity – Lars Hultberg. Unknown to us that is, but not to Bernie Persson. The young Swede was a team-mate of Persson's at his Scandinavian club and came highly recommended by the Cradley skipper.

But what of the old guard? Roy Trigg was transferred to Newport, Mick Handley to Swindon, and dear old Squibby had decided to chance his arm in the new National League. Would he ever retire? Bob Andrews elected to stay in New Zealand and retired from British League racing. All four had given good service and all would have a place in the hearts of the Heathens supporters for many years to come. United began the season with a couple of challenge matches at Cradley in March. Persson and Hultberg were not due in England until the end of the month, but at least the matches would 'break in' three of the new boys. The Heathens won the first, against Sheffield, but lost the second to Leicester (as usual).

Their first League match was at Swindon and a full-strength Cradley team earned a draw. Cole top-scored with 10 points and Hultberg made a promising British debut, scoring 4 points. A home win against Halifax saw Persson score his first maximum of the season. Cribb supported well by scoring 10 points, as did Cole with 8. Jarman and Perks scored 4 points each and Hultberg scored 3. Goody had an off night and failed to score, but it was a very encouraging all-round performance.

The Heathens paid their first visit of the season to Monmore Green at the beginning of April. Wolves' new signing, Wee Georgie Hunter from Scotland, combined well with Olsen to lead the home side to an 8-point victory. The two Wolverhampton stars were unbeaten by a Heathen and Persson failed in his attempt to relieve Ole of the Golden Helmet, but considering that Jarman had two engine failures, Cribb fell and Perks and Cole were excluded, Cradley might well have been on the other end of that scoreline.

However, United were back to winning ways the following night, and despite two engine failures by Persson, Cradley still beat Coventry 45-33. Cole top-scored with 13 points, and in the return at Brandon the following Saturday, he collected his first Cradley maximum, leading the Heathens to an impressive 14-point win away from home. Howard was fully justifying the faith that the Cradley management had placed in him when they signed him from the injured list. Never the best gater in the world, he had to score most of his points from the back, and after a handful of matches, Cole was challenging Bernie Persson for the title of 'Most Popular Heathen'. In fact, the pair linked up to win the LP Transport Best Pairs Trophy at Dudley Wood against such opposition as Olsen and Hunter.

Harry Bastable was walking around with his chest sticking out and his head held high – and so he should have done, as he had been right. He had already saved Cradley on the track as a rider in 1960, and now he was doing it again as their manager some thirteen years later. The squad had the team spirit that he said he would instil into them at the beginning of the season. They were supporting one another, helping one another out in the pits and it was spilling over onto the track. When one had a bad

1973 team line-up. From left to right, back row: Howard Cole, Lars Hultberg, Harry Bastable (manager), Pete Jarman, Colin Goody. Front: Dave Perks, Dave Harvey, Bernt Persson. (www.mike-patrick.com)

meeting, the others would be up there scoring points to cover him. It could have been Goody, Jarman or Cribb, but someone always seemed to be there to plug the holes.

Cradley beat Swindon by 18 points at Dudley Wood, and with Persson having a below-par night, young Dave Perks came through, winning two races and beating the Robins' number one, Martin Ashby, in the process. The Heathens saw out April in second place in the League behind Leicester. Persson was scoring well, as were Cole and Goody. Jarman and Cribb were inconsistent, but Pete could be a match-winner on the night, and Cribby would only get better as the season progressed. Dave Perks was obviously a star of the future, and Lars Hultberg was just as good as Bernie had said he would be. Cradley were on the crest of a wave – and then it all went horribly wrong.

In Cradley's last home fixture in April, they held off a strong challenge by Hackney to win the match by 4 points, but Howard Cole crashed in the second half, breaking his ankle and dislocating his shoulder – a three month lay-off at best. Cole was a heat-leader and the Heathens would be allowed to use guests to replace him if they so desired, but Howard was as popular in the pits as he was on the terraces, and there was no doubt in anyone's mind that his presence would be sadly missed by the rest of the boys.

Cradley's next meeting was the Midland Riders' Championship qualifying round, and the Heathens gave the fans something to cheer when Goody and Persson finished on top of the pile with 13 points each. However, Cradley's next team performance saw their run of success come to an abrupt halt, as despite a stunning 18-point maximum from Bernie, the Heathens lost their home leg of a Knockout Cup match by 4 points to Poole. In this year it was decided to run the preliminary round on a home and away basis, so at least they would have another bite of the cherry.

The troops rallied, but lost their next match at the County Ground to a very strong Exeter side led by their new signing, Ivan Mauger. Guest Bob Valentine managed only 2 points, and it was left to Persson and Cribb to supply the opposition. United won their next encounter at Brandon, thanks to a Persson maximum, but the match was marred by a terrible accident suffered by the Bees' Les Owen, who was taken to hospital in a critical condition. The Heathens were forced to count the cost too as Goody broke his collarbone in the second half of the meeting, leaving Cradley with two men on the injured list and one gremlin well and truly back from vacation.

When League leaders Reading visited Dudley Wood, they faced a very strange-looking United side, with only Perks, Cribb and Hultberg being present. Guests Barry Thomas and Arnold Hayley did well, but Roger Johns and Graham Stapleton scored only 2 points between them and the Heathens lost by a massive 18 points. Harry Bastable strove to maintain the team spirit, and he must have motivated young Hultberg, for he scored 9 points at Halifax and was bettered only by Persson and guest George Hunter with 10 points each. Even so, the other four (who included junior Dave Harvey) failed to respond and the Heathens lost by 10 points.

In their last match of May, Cradley were knocked out of the Knockout Cup at Poole, Colin Goody having made a comeback to the team. However, it was one of the shortest comebacks in history, for just five nights later, as the Heathens beat Coventry to move into the next round of the Midland Cup, Colin did his collarbone again and was out for another two weeks. Cradley won their next home fixture against Newport, but it was to be their last League win for three months! They played host to Oxford one week later and lost by 2 points, but the score paled into insignificance as they lost Cribb with a fractured leg and Hultberg with a broken shoulder. Hultberg was reckoned to be out for a month, but for Bruce Cribb, the season was over. With Cole and Goody still sidelined, the Heathens were decimated.

Goody made a welcome return at the beginning of July, and Cradley went through the motions, using a series of guests from both the British and National Leagues, but only Persson was riding like he hadn't had the stuffing knocked out of him. The

Dave Perks. (Speedway Star)

Malcolm Corradine. (Speedway Star)

Heathens were losing all of their League matches and were tumbling down the League table. Cole made his return to Dudley Wood, the same night as Hultberg, in Cradley's last match of July, in which they beat a Midland Select team. Howard scored 8 points, and looked like he'd never been away, but Lars looked out of touch, scoring a solitary point.

Young Dave Harvey had put in some gutsy performances since being bought into the team, but he could hardly have been expected to fill Cribby's shoes, and with Persson missing the odd match due to Swedish commitments, the Heathens lost every match in August. Every one except one that is – the second leg of the Dudley/Wolves Trophy. Cradley had lost the Wolverhampton leg by only 6 points, and must have fancied their chances in the return, but they won at Dudley Wood by only 2 points, and the Trophy went back to Monmore Green

In an attempt to boost flagging morale, Bastable signed Malcolm Corradine from National League Birmingham for £1,000. He had guested for United a few weeks earlier, scoring 8 points at Leicester, and impressing Harry into the bargain. He arrived at the beginning of September, but only managed to get close to that score on one occasion before the season ended.

Halfway through the month, Cradley won their first League match for over three months when they beat Kings Lynn at Dudley Wood. It was to be their last win of the season, as they remained stuck at the bottom of the League.

The only thing that the Heathens fans had to get excited about was Bernie's third consecutive appearance in a World Final, this time in Poland. In effect, they had little to celebrate, as the Swede fell in his first race, failed to finish in two others, and finished in last place, typifying Cradley's dreadful season. This was the famous World Final that saw some dubious refereeing, and Poland produced their first ever World Champion in Jerzy Szczakiel, after Mauger had fallen in a run-off with him for the title.

Persson returned and top scored in a couple of meetings before he was off on his travels again to compete in the Swedish Riders Championship. He had made his last appearance in Cradley colours for quite some time. News filtered back from Sweden that there had been an accident in the final. Bernie Persson had broken his arm and would not be able to ride again in 1973.

Bastable, never one to quit on the track, applied the same attitude to his managerial duties, and immediately sought a replacement for his number one. He came up with the Norwegian Ulf Lovaas. Ulf's brother Dag had made quite a name for himself at Reading that season, and although, Ulf had ridden only two meetings in 1973,due to National Service, he was keen to join the Heathens for the rest of the season.

He made his debut at Leicester at the beginning of October in the Midland Cup Semi-Final, and although United lost heavily he looked impressive, scoring 7 points. In their next match, Cradley visited Oxford and scored a mere 19 points, losing Cole for the rest of the season after a spill in his first outing. There seemed to be no end to the Heathens' wretched luck.

Cradley were into the guest situation once again for the rest of the season, but in the final two matches, Lovaas top scored, with Dave Perks just behind him – maybe there was something to look forward to in 1974. It had been an awful year for the Heathens. It had been another season that had promised so much, and yielded so little. They had had the most diabolical year imaginable.

The team spirit that Bastable had worked so hard to achieve had crumbled. No team spirit would have survived what Cradley went through in 1973. Jarman, rarely mentioned in this chapter, rode for a long period of time with a broken finger, and Goody had returned to the team before he was even half-fit more than once. Cole had looked as though he was in for his best season ever, and was robbed by cruel injuries, not once but twice, but he still finished with an average of over 9 points per match. Bruce Cribb was not so fortunate – he never got two bites, only one – and then he was gone. Indestructible Bernie Persson had seen his average fall by 1.5 points and had a poor year by his own impeccable standards before becoming another victim of the Cradley gremlin.

Dave Perks was frankly disappointing after such a favourable start the previous year, but time was on his side and the way he ended the season indicated that the next year he should be one of the leading lights at Dudley Wood. Lars Hultberg failed to make the grade; injury and the problems that surrounded the team were too much for his young head and his form reflected that. Young Dave Harvey had done everything that had been asked of him in his debut year in the British League, but he needed more time.

There had been a wind of change in the British League in 1973. A Polish World Champion, a Norwegian finishing in sixth place in the British League averages – Dag Lovaas – and a new top man in the League, the dynamic Swede, Anders Michanek, who topped the British League averages ahead of Mauger and Olsen and led Reading to the League title. It had been a diabolical year for Bastable in his managerial debut, yet never once did he falter. He watched proudly as his team challenged for the League leader-ship, only to see them crumble before his eyes and plummet to the very foot of the League table, ravaged by injury. The fact that he had bought young Corradine was testimony that Harry was looking to the future – a future that would hopefully hold better fortune for the Heathens. Harry had been right about the change of name, it had bought about a change of fortune, but no one could possibly have expected it to be for the worse.

21

THE AUSTRALIAN PLUMBER
1974

Aruling by the Control Board in the winter had a direct bearing on Cradley's line-up for 1974. It had been decreed that there would be no commuting foreigners allowed in the British League. That meant that any foreigner that had to return home and miss British League fixtures would not be allowed to ride in Britain. In other words, there would be no Anders Michanek, Bengt Jansson, Tommy Jansson or Christer Lofqvist. For Cradley, it meant meant no Bernie Persson! At least Persson was recognised by Rider Allocation for what he was – one of the top riders in the sport – and he was replaced by a rider that had enjoyed an even more prolific 1973 season, the current Midland Riders' Champion, John Boulger.

The twenty-eight-year-old former Australian Champion had begun his British career with Long Eaton in 1967 and when they closed, he moved with rest of the team to Leicester where he had stayed until he was allocated to Cradley. The former Aussie plumber already had one World final appearance under his belt, and had finished the 1973 season with an average of over 10 points a match. In other words, John was hot and whilst Bernie had slipped a little the previous season, Boulger was on the up-and-up. The Heathens' supporters could certainly not complain about Persson's replacement.

There were other changes too. Colin Goody had moved on to Poole and Pete Jarman had moved down to the National League with Eastbourne. Ulf Lovaas, who many thought would be on Cradley's shopping list after his efforts in 1973, lined up with Oxford. The management had pulled off quite a coup by signing National League Boston's Arthur Price. Twenty-eight-year-old Arthur was the reigning National League Riders' Champion and was reckoned to have the brightest of futures ahead of him. The Heathens had also signed a team-mate of Price's at Boston, Russell Osborne. The 'old guard' was to be Cole, Cribb, Perks and Corradine.

The speedway season began with the country in disarray. The miners' strike had led to power cuts across the length and breadth of the land, and many of the fixtures in March had been cancelled, including a challenge match between Cradley and Swindon. The Heathens finally managed to open the season later that month with a couple of challenge matches at Dudley Wood. The first one was a convincing win against Sheffield, with Ray Wilson, who was standing in for Boulger, scoring a maximum. John was not due in England until the following week. Cole dropped only 1 point and Perks and Price supported admirably.

The second match was against a very strong Belle Vue team, which Cradley lost. Boulger arrived late and missed his first ride, but he still managed to score 7 points. Price top-scored with 9 points, but the star of the night was young Perky, picking up 8 points and beating whiz kid Peter Collins into the bargain. Cole was forced to withdraw from the meeting following a fall in his second outing, which left the supporters praying that this season had not begun as last year's had ended.

Four nights later, the serious stuff started as United went to Brandon to face Coventry in the first round of the Midland Cup. Boulger was well known as a Brandon track specialist and Cradley looked to him for some fireworks, but John was plagued by machine troubles and scored only 5 points. However, the Heathens did hold the Bees to a draw, thanks to a brilliant maximum by Dave Perks. Russell Osborne was also a revelation, scoring 7 points from the reserve berth. It was just as well because Cole was still in pain and struggled, managing only 2 points.

Cradley thrashed Coventry in the return at Dudley Wood and this time Arthur Price was the star, scoring his first ever British League maximum. Cole was back to his best and Boulger was getting his bikes sorted out, so it was no surprise when the Heathens took the points at Kings Lynn in their first League match of the season in mid-April. United were brought down to earth with a bump at Monmore Green when Wolves beat them by 18 points in the first leg of the Knockout Cup. In the return leg, Cradley could only manage a 2-point win and made an early exit from the competition. Ominous Ole Olsen was unbeaten in both legs.

The Heathens enjoyed a comfortable home win against Swindon before getting a drubbing at Newport, where Malcolm Corradine, who was having a fine match, fell and sustained facial injuries, becoming became the first Heathen on the 1974 injury list. In an effort to fill the gap, Cradley brought in ex-England international Dave Younghusband. Thirty-six-year-old Dave had retired two years previously after breaking his leg, but the Heathens fans still remembered him riding for Halifax when he was the scourge of Dudley Wood. During the late 1960s, no Cradley rider beat him for years. Dave started off a little tentatively at first, scoring only 1 point in each of his first two matches, but considering his performances at Dudley Wood in the past, the management were prepared to persevere.

Boulger was now hitting top form and won the British Airways Silver Jubilee Trophy at Coventry, following that achievement with a sizzling 15-point maximum as he led the Heathens to victory at Hull. He gated behind Dave Gifford and Bobby Beaton in the last race, and the manner in which he shot under Beaton to claim his fifth win brought a storm of protest from Hull's manager, Ian Thomas, but it was to no avail and United took the points. Scarcely had the celebrations begun when tragedy befell the Heathens. Dave Perks fell in the second half and broke his leg.

Once again, with Cradley riding high in second place in the League, they had been struck down by injury. A shiver went through Cole and Cribb, who had been subject to the horrors of 1973. Could it all be happening again? Harry Bastable must have wished that there was something that he could do out there on the track. He couldn't ride himself, so he did the next best thing – he put his son, Steve, into the team.

Steve had made his debut at Dudley Wood the previous season in the Opportunity

1974 programme cover.

Stakes, and had continued to do well in 1974. He looked a cracking prospect, a real chip off the old block in fact. Still, his debut at the end of April was premature, and the single point that he scored, as Cradley beat Poole at Dudley Wood, was only by virtue of the opposition's rider falling. But at just seventeen years old, Steve had time on his side and without a doubt his day would come. Dave Younghusband seemed to be about to repay the management's faith in him in that match, scoring 6 points, but after another three pointless matches, he too joined the injury list with a nasty-sounding injury to his rear end. It spelled the end of the line for Dave and he retired from speedway.

Cradley entered May with Corradine back in the team, but in his second match, at Dudley Wood against Wolverhampton in the first leg of the Midland Cup semi-final, he retired from the meeting after only one race, deciding that his comeback had been premature. United lost the fixture by 14 points to the old enemy, and the telltale cracks began to appear. Boulger was the only Heathen to show any consistency. He won the World Championship qualifying round at Hull and seemed to be going from strength to strength. Skipper Cole was, in the main, riding well, but he had the odd match when he would score only 1 or 2 points. Cribby was, without doubt, the most inconsistent rider in the team. Would he score 10 or would he score 2? You just never knew.

Cradley could be pleased with Arthur Price. He had started off like a whirling dervish but had settled down to being a 6-point man, which was no mean feat for his first full term in the British League. Russell Osborne could not be faulted for his efforts either, but he was sharing his time between Cradley and Boston and was not always available. However, consistency is the name of the game and the Heathens were sadly lacking on this front. United failed to win a match in May. Cole missed a couple of matches with 'flu and Cradley called upon Steve Bastable, who was now riding for Stoke in the National League. They tried a succession of other NL boys as well, but they were out of their depth at this level.

Johnny Boulger continued to enjoy himself, winning the World Pairs semi-final with Phil Crump in Germany and qualifying for the British final. The Heathens' only creditable performance in May was their last match of the month at Monmore, when they lost by only 2 points. Granted, they were out of the Midland Cup, but Price made the night a bit special when he beat Olsen in heat ten.

Corradine made a more successful comeback in June and settled into low-order scoring, but a rare off night by Boulger got Cradley off to a bad start to the month, losing at home to Ipswich. In their next match, at Dudley Wood, Oxford were the visitors, but just before things got underway, the area was hit by a power cut. The starting tapes had to be operated by battery and a red flag was used in place of the track stoplights. Under these circumstances, the Cheetahs insisted that the match be run as a challenge rather than a League encounter. Just as well really, as United could only scrape a draw.

Bastable (senior) decided that something had to be done to strengthen the team, and he set about looking for another rider. With the Swedes 'banned', riders were thin on the ground, so Harry went for another 'retiree', ex-Hungarian Freedom Fighter, Sandor Levai. Sandor had been one of the great characters of the sport and had seen action at Stoke, Norwich and Belle Vue, but at nearly fifty years of age, was it the right time to bring him back to speedway? The Hungarian joined the side in the middle of June, but understandably took his time getting match-fit again. United lost their next three matches, making it twelve defeats in a row. The season was taking on a remarkable resemblance to the previous disastrous year, as Cradley spiralled down the League table.

Boulger still seemed unaffected by the carnage going on around him. He scored an 18-point maximum at Halifax, a 15-point maximum at Leicester, finished in fourth place in the British final and picked up his second individual trophy at Sheffield when he won the Yorkshire Bank Trophy. Steve Bastable was letting his dad do all the worrying. He was improving week by week at Stoke, and picked up the runner-up spot in the Junior Championship of the British Isles behind winner Chris Morton. A few weeks later, he made Harry cough up £100 for beating the old man's 1960 track record of 71.6 seconds in a second-half race at Dudley Wood.

Towards the end of the month, the team clicked at Cradley when the Heathens played host to Wimbledon Dons. Osborne and Levai both scored well, and Cradley showed what they could do when they won the match by an impressive 20 points. They ended June with two away defeats, Cole missing with tonsillitis.

July proved to be a strange month for the Heathens. They began by losing at Exeter, but Boulger scored a sensational 15-point maximum that included a win over Ivan

1974 team line-up. Malcolm Corradine, John Boulger, Bruce Cribb, Howard Cole (on machine), Harry Bastable (manager), Arthur Price, Russell Osborne, Dave Perks, Sandor Levai. (www.mike-patrick.com)

Howard Colt and Sandor Levai. (Speedway Star)

Mauger. Cradley followed this with a win at Dudley Wood against Coventry, a defeat at Dudley Wood against Kings Lynn, a win away at Oxford, and finished off the month with defeats at home to Belle Vue and Oxford!

Meanwhile, Johnny Boulger was on a roll. He came second in the Brandonapolis at Coventry, sandwiched in between Mauger and Olsen, and with partner Crump, he finished runner-up in the World Pairs Championship to Sweden's Anders Michanek and Soren Sjosten. He collected his third trophy when he won the Holiday Cup from Terry Betts and Norman Hunter at Leicester, and he also won the Midland Riders' qualifying round at Dudley Wood. Amidst the gloom, Cradley had a world-class star in every sense of the word.

United opened their August account with a win at Dudley Wood, against Hull, followed by a defeat at Cradley against Leicester. The Lions' rising star Dave Jessup was superb, scoring a brilliant maximum and leading Leicester to a 2-point win. In heat one, he inflicted Boulger's only defeat of the night, and lowered the track record to 66.2 seconds in the process.

The month was disappointing for Boulger when an engine failure prevented him from qualifying for the British/Nordic final stage of the World Championship, and he made the European final only as reserve. However, he then represented Australia in the

Arthur Price. (Speedway Star)

World Team Cup final, in which they were runners-up to England, and won the Midland Riders' qualifying round at Leicester. He returned to Blackbird Road one week later to win the Golden Gauntlets Trophy, but realistically his chance at the big one, the World Championship, was over for another year.

By the end of the month, Cradley were three from the bottom of the League table, but they ended August in the best way possible by taking the League points at Monmore Green. Olsen was unbeaten, but the Heathens scored solidly throughout the team to win by a single point.

170

September was a quiet month for Cradley with only three home matches, all of which they won, including the first leg of the Dudley/Wolves Trophy. But the big news in September was that Anders Michanek was the new World Champion. He took the title in Gothenburg from Mauger and Sjosten, perhaps proving that the British League needed the Swedes more than the Swedes needed the British League. The Golden Helmet had been run in a different format in 1974. Previously, the holder defended it every match against the top-scorer from the opposing team. The Control Board deemed this to be unfair and decided that the Helmet would from now on be defended on a monthly basis. The challenger would be nominated by the Board and the Match Race Championship would be contested over the best of three races at the holder's track and then at the challenger's track, and if the results were level, the best of three at a neutral track. John Boulger was named as the October challenger for Aussie team-mate Phil Crump's Golden Helmet. John won 2-1 at Cradley, lost 1-2 at Newport, and then lost 1-2 at Wimbledon. Crumpie took the Helmet into the close season, but not without a fight.

Dave Perks came back at the end of September, just as Malcolm Corradine left for Long Eaton, but there was not enough of the season for Perky to re-establish himself, and for Dave it had been a wasted year. Cradley finished off the season by beating Leicester at Dudley Wood for the first time since the formation of the British League, albeit in a challenge match, and they also won the Dudley/Wolves Trophy. Unfortunately, they set a new record too. Their 62-16 defeat at Sheffield was the biggest defeat ever recorded in the British League!

United finished thirteenth in a league of seventeen teams, the overall winners being Exeter. True, it was an improvement on the previous year, but hardly a record to be proud of. Johnny Boulger was a star. He did what he was brought in to do and replaced Persson with ease. He finished the year with an average of 10.06 points, his nearest rival being Cole with a disappointing 7.70 points.

Bruce Cribb had stayed in the middle, averaging 6.29 points. He had proved himself to be an important team-man for the Heathens – he was never an 'attention grabber', but was always scoring points. Arthur Price had begun the year looking as though he could be the signing of the season, but as the team spirit wavered, so did his consistency. However, he still had a fairly good debut year in the British League and averaged 5.56 points.

Sandor Levai had done a good job. He had been brought out of retirement at the age of fifty into the strongest speedway League in the world, and he still managed to average 5.79 points. If not for Sandor, Cradley may well have been the 1974 wooden spoonists. Russell Osborne had been a success at reserve and his 4.7 point average was a credit to him in his first year at Dudley Wood. It had been another tough season for riders and supporters alike. Cradley fought as hard as anyone for success, but they never got the breaks. The fans must have wondered if success would ever come to their unlucky club.

22

THE FOUR VALVES ARRIVE
1975

There was plenty going on prior to the start of the 1975 season. Reading, after being absent for twelve months, elected to return to the British League. This led the Control Board, fearing a shortage of riders, to relax their ban on the Swedes. It also meant the World Champion Anders Michanek would be racing in England again. Ole Olsen was in dispute with Wolverhampton after requesting a transfer, which they understandably refused. His name was at one stage linked with Oxford, but as the season began, he lined up for neither club and one wondered if he had been lost to the sport.

Perhaps the biggest news, although it was not regarded as such by some at the time, was that Phil Crump and his father-in-law (veteran Neil Street) were on their way from Australia to ride for Newport on their 'super bikes'. The machines had four valves and were a conversion job that Street had developed in the winter. Such information went straight over the heads of most speedway fans because unlike most other motor sports, ninety-nine per cent of speedway fans know nothing about motorbikes. Speedway has always been, and always will be, about the riders and not their machinery, but such was the impact of this new innovation in the sport that the term 'four valve' was heard at every track around the country.

The big news at Cradley, of course, was that Bernie Persson was coming back to Dudley Wood, joining Johnny Boulger to form one of the most potent warheads in the league. Also returning were Price, Cribb, Levai, Perks and Osborne. The only other change was that Harry Bastable had left to take over as co-promoter at Stoke, where he could keep an eye on his son Steve. Peter Worthington was named as the new Cradley manager. He must have prayed that the run of bad luck that had plagued Harry throughout his two years in the post at Dudley Wood was not going to continue.

Missing, of course, was Howard Cole. He had always enjoyed his winters in Australia, and after becoming completely disillusioned with speedway in the British League, he decided to emigrate to Oz and went with Cradley's best wishes. The Heathens were due to open at Dudley Wood on 15 March, but their challenge match against Sheffield was cancelled due to rain and snow. They got underway one week later, beating Wimbledon at Cradley in a challenge match that saw Persson and Boulger slip comfortably back into the groove.

The last Friday in the month saw them at Monmore Green, but they lost to an Olsen-less Wolves by 6 points. The following night at Dudley Wood, the Heathens began their

League campaign with an 8-point win over Swindon, and two nights later, they lost by just 3 points at Coventry in the first round of the Midland Cup.

It was an encouraging start, and all of the lads were riding well, but in their first match in April, at Oxford, Cradley recorded the lowest ever score in a British League match when they lost 14-58 (beating their own record set the previous year). The weather was absolutely dire, and the Heathens complained to the referee about the state of the track a number of times in the first few races. He apparently saw nothing wrong with riding while it was snowing, but following a blizzard after heat seven, Cradley withdrew from the meeting and Oxford continued, putting out both of their riders and winning every subsequent heat 5-0.

The Heathens' next match at Dudley Wood was a milestone. They beat Leicester for the first time ever in a British League match! Cribb led the assault with 11 points, followed by Boulger (8), Levai (6), Persson (6), Osborne (4), Perks (4) and Price (3). Even so, nobody beat Dave Jessup as he roared to another 15-point maximum.

United made their way through April winning at home and losing away. As expected, Boulger and Persson frequently top-scored, but John had not yet captured the form he showed in 1974 and Bernie was not the Bernie of old. Cribb was steady, on around 6 points a match, and Levai and Osborne were putting in the occasional good performance, but Perks was finding the points hard to come by on the away tracks. On the other hand, Arthur Price was coming good. He top-scored a couple of times in April and was challenging for the third heat-leader spot.

May began incredibly well. Cradley visited the County Ground and beat league champions Exeter by an amazing 18 points. Ivan Mauger scored a 15-point maximum, and although the Falcons lost Scott Autrey prior to the match with an asthma attack, this should not detract from a superb Heathens display. Price, Boulger and Cribb all scored double figures, but it was an all-round team performance that ended Exeter's run of 31 consecutive home wins. United continued the month with a win at National League Teeside in the Inter-Divisional Cup and a brilliant League win at Kings Lynn, in which Boulger scored a maximum and Steve Bastable, in for Osborne, scored a well-earned 6 points. United were in second place in the League table, but the fans were cautious – they had seen it all before.

Russell Osborne had decided that the British League was not for him – which was a pity, for he had given some fine performances for the Heathens – and he had returned to the National League. Bastable, who was really piling up the points for Stoke, had agreed to appear for Cradley, depending on availability, if they required his services. This turned out to be a rash decision by Steve as he turned out be required for the rest of the season!

Ole Olsen had finally agreed terms with Wolverhampton and he quickly showed that his late start to the season had not given the other riders any advantage whatsoever, as he stormed to a 15-point maximum in Cradley's qualifying round of the Midland Riders' Championship. It was a good night for the Heathens too, with Boulger taking second place with 14 points and Persson taking third with 12 points. Bastable and Cribb were joint fifth with 9 points. In May. when Persson and Boulger were forced to miss four matches between them due to international duties, Cradley began to have an unsettled

1975 programme cover.

look about them. This coincided with a purple patch of form for Price. Although the Heathens lost at Halifax and Wolverhampton, Arthur top-scored with double figures in both, finishing the month with a win in Cradley's qualifying round of the World Championship. He was rewarded with a short tour of Poland with the England squad. It was both Arthur's first time out of the country and in an aeroplane, and while it must have been the experience of a lifetime for him, he was sorely missed in United's next two matches as they went into June.

The first match was a home encounter with Exeter, who were without Ivan Mauger. Cradley, on the other hand, were without Persson, who was busy finishing third in the Intercontinental final. Mauger won that meeting, but the Heathens' other World final hope, Boulger, crashed out with only 4 points. Cradley scraped a 2-point win, thanks to Steve Bastable, who top-scored with 12 points. With their top men on World Championship duty, both teams were allowed a guest rider, and while Bob Humphreys did well for the Heathens (scoring 8 points), Phil Crump, on his four-valve, seemed head and shoulders above any other rider on the night and rattled off an untroubled maximum.

Ole Olsen won the Midlands Riders' Championship at Brandon and Boulger was Cradley's top representative, finishing in fourth place, but Price and Cribb finished way down the bottom of the field. Persson made his return for the next match at Hackney, but the single point that he scored did little to help their cause as the Heathens only managed to scrape 20 points. In their next fixture at Dudley Wood, against Wimbledon, Cradley had booked Birmingham's Arthur Browning, as Bastable was unavailable. Arthur withdrew his services at the last moment when the Cradley management refused to pay him £200. Browning claimed that they had agreed to pay him this amount when he loaned his bike to Bruce Cribb two years ago when Bruce had fallen, broken his leg and extensively damaged Arthur's bike into the bargain. The management denied any such agreement, told Browning to get on *his* bike, and brought in junior Paul Share.

Paul was outclassed, as were most of the Heathens in this match, and the Dons won by a comfortable 8 points. Boulger was sadly missed, competing in the World Pairs final in Poland with partner Phil Crump. The Aussies had to settle for fifth place in the competition, which was again won by Sweden. United progressed to the second round of the Knockout Cup by beating Kings Lynn on aggregate, and failed by only 7 points in the first leg of the Midland Cup semi-final at Wolves. In their last match of the month, Cradley lost by 10 points at Coventry – this was not a bad result considering that Persson arrived too late to take his place in the match. Bernie had been to Sweden and had decided to return by road in order to collect his very own new four-valve machine on his way back to Britain. The real sickener was that whilst he was making his way to Brandon Stadium, Dave Perks was leaving the track in an ambulance with a broken collarbone.

Regarding the four-valve machines, the manufacturers had all jumped on the bandwagon, and four-valvers, although not yet readily available, could at least be ordered. They were expensive to buy and apparently expensive to maintain and repair, but in order to keep in the hunt, the riders just had to have them. Persson had the repu-

1975 team line-up. From left to right: Bernt Persson, Dave Perks, Bruce Cribb, Russell Osborne, John Boulger (on machine), Sandor Levai, Arthur Price, Peter Worthington (manager). (www.mike-patrick.com)

tation of striking a hard bargain when it came to signing new contracts, but by the same token, he spared no expense on his equipment, and it came as no surprise that he was the first Heathen to acquire one of these mean machines.

In his first meeting at Dudley Wood astride his new bike, Bernie scored a maximum against a poor Coventry side, but in his next match at Ipswich, his new bike gave him problems and he scored only 4 points, as Cradley lost by 8 points at Foxhall Heath. Boulger and Cribb were superb for United, and showed the same form at Dudley Wood a couple of nights later when Cradley were unlucky not to beat League leaders Belle Vue. The Heathens did manage a draw, however, but engine failures for both Boulger and Persson undoubtedly cost Cradley the match.

United lost their last four matches in July: a challenge match at Hull, which saw Boulger and the Vikings' team manager, Derek Tattershall, almost come to blows; two League defeats (home and away) against Reading; and an Inter-Divisional Knockout Cup match at Oxford, which saw them exit from the competition. The League defeats against Reading were both a case of bad luck. Cradley, despite Perks' absence and Bastable's occasional unavailability, were riding well, but Bernie's bike let him down again at Dudley Wood. At Smallmead, only an engine failure by Boulger and an exclusion by Cribb prevented the Heathens from pulling off the shock result of the season, in a match that saw Cribb beat World Champion Michanek.

Cradley rode into August thrashing Hull at Dudley Wood before travelling to Newport for the second round of the Knockout Cup. Crump and Street were both unbeaten on their 'super bikes' and the Heathens were thumped 49-29. No one gave United much chance in the return leg the following night at Cradley Heath, but this time, Persson was unbeaten and this time Crump and Street experienced engine failures. The Heathens all pulled together, pulled back the deficit, and went on to win the tie by 4 points on aggregate. This was no mean feat considering that Newport were challenging for the League leadership, and Cradley had lost Levai in the very first heat of the match. Perks had made a useful return, scoring 7 points, but as he came back, Sandor went out.

The problems were now coming thick and fast. Over the previous few weeks, Cradley had used a succession of National League riders to cover for Perks without much return. When they had finally managed to assemble their full team, against Newport, the formation had not lasted a single race. Levai had broken his collarbone and his season was over. The pace had finally got to young Bastable and he told the Cradley management 'No more'. The pressure of riding for two teams and the travelling involved were proving too much for him – suddenly, Cradley were looking at only half a team. Some fast talking persuaded Steve to continue giving his services to United when he was not riding for Stoke, and he continued to thrash himself mentally and physically until the end of the season.

In mid-August, Exeter held the Heathens to a draw at Dudley Wood, and it was very much the Ivan Mauger show. At the age of thirty-five, the New Zealander seemed to be having his best ever season. In his first race, he equalled the track record, and then proceeded to fire off another four successive wins. It was 16 August and, incredibly, Ivan had dropped only 4 League points all year! One week later, the Kiwi won the European final after a run-off with Olsen. Persson was also there and booked his place in yet another World final. However, it was to be another poor World final for Bernie, finishing tenth with 5 points, but the biggest shock was that Mauger did not make the rostrum and had to settle for fourth place behind new Champion Ole Olsen, Anders Michanek and England's John Louis.

Cradley finished August with some very strange looking line-ups, Persson being on duty in Sweden. His absence was too much for the Heathens and they lost three away matches and the Dudley/Wolves Trophy into

Sandor Levai. (Speedway Star)

Dave Perks and John Boulger. (Speedway Star)

the bargain Cradley fared a little better in September, winning three British League matches and losing two. They lost at home by 2 points to the eventual League Champions, Ipswich, but the highlight of the month was an away win at Swindon, in which Arthur Price scored an immaculate maximum. Towards the end of the month, it was cup-tie time at Dudley Wood, but it was not a very successful time as far as the Heathens were concerned. They lost the first leg of the Knockout Cup semi-final by 13 points to Belle Vue, and lost the second leg of the Midland Cup semi-final to Wolverhampton, thus making their exit from the competition.

United began October by getting knocked out of the Knockout Cup at Belle Vue, but they then had a good win at home against Newport, winning by 13 points and putting paid to the Wasps' League title hopes. Cradley finished the season by winning two matches at Dudley Wood – a challenge match against Leicester and a League match against Wolves, which the Heathens won by 22 points. Persson inflicted a rare defeat upon Ole Olsen.

When the dust had settled and thoughts had been collected, it had not been Cradley's worst year by any means. They finished in eleventh place in a league of eighteen teams, but there had been something missing. It was certainly not great racing that was missing as the Dudley Wood track had a reputation for being one of the fairest and finest in the League. The supporters, more often than not, were treated to one thrilling match after another, hence United's famous support which existed even in the lean times.

What they lacked in 1975 was a hero. Most people suspected that it would be Boulger or Persson, whilst others thought that Dave Perks would be the one to draw them through the turnstiles week after week, but in reality it was neither. Perks had a nightmare of a season. He began slowly, broke his collarbone and returned to show indifferent form. True, there were occasional flashes of brilliance, the brilliance that everyone knew that he possessed, but at the end of the season, he found himself at the bottom of the Heathens averages and he must have been glad to see the back of 1975.

At the other end of the scale, John Boulger topped the Heathens' averages, but 8.73 points was not even high enough to put him in the British League Riders' final. John had dropped his average by almost $1\frac{1}{2}$ points from the previous year and had not been the force that he was in 1974. Persson was also a disappointment. His frequent visits to Sweden had got on everyone's nerves and had cost the team its equilibrium. He finished with an 8-point average.

Just 1 point per match down on Bernie was Arthur Price, who had lacked consistency, but had scored four maximums and had taken over the third heat-leader spot – Price had a fine season. Bruce Cribb finished just behind Arthur, and quite frankly should not have done. He undoubtedly had the skill and talent to be a 9-point man, and indeed sometimes was, but those times were not regular enough, and Cribby found himself ousted from the heat-leader trio. The old 'un and the young 'un were next – there was nothing between Levai and Bastable, with an average of just less than 5 points a match. Sandor gave his all, only to be sidelined by injury at the end of the season. Steve gave more than his all and nearly cracked up in doing so.

23

THE KIWI COMES GOOD
1976

Cradley went into 1976 with almost the same squad with which they had ended 1975. Sandor Levai had decided to retire to build up his garage business and, come the start of the season, he stuck to his guns. The Heathens already had a man halfway through to the World Final in skipper Johnny Boulger. During the winter, he had won the Australian Championship and had, due to the new qualifying system, already booked himself a place in the Intercontinental final.

Stevie B was back, this time on a full-time basis, having elected to leave Stoke and take up British League racing exclusively. Bruce Cribb and Arthur Price had re-signed, and the punters waited to see if Price could continue the progress that he made the previous year, as well as if Cribb could show the consistency that would forge Cradley into a 'serious' outfit. Dave Perks returned from a winter spent racing in New Zealand and was boasting a new K680 Westlake machine with a Neil Street four-valve conversion. Evergreen Swede Bernie Persson was back, and the fans just hoped that they would see more of him than they had done in the previous year. Twenty-one-year-old Nigel Wasley had been with Perks in Kiwiland, and he was brought in from National League Crewe to complete the Heathens line-up.

There was yet another change in the managerial department – involving another ex-Heathen – when Vic White made a comeback to Dudley Wood. Previously, White had managed Leicester and had proved himself to be astute and knowledgeable in every aspect of the game. Many of the supporters still remembered Vic's hair-raising antics around the Cradley track back in the early 1960s. Much would depend on Persson and Boulger 'raising their game' after a somewhat disappointing season for both in 1975. Bastable looked certain to improve, in fact he was reckoned to be one of the hottest prospects around, and surely this year would be Perks' year.

As the season began, two events that indirectly involved Cradley should be mentioned. Birmingham had moved up from the National League to take their place alongside the 'big boys' in the British League – someone to take Wolverhampton's place as the arch-enemy? And speaking of United's beloved foes, World Champion Ole Olsen had finally got his wish and left Monmore for Coventry.

Dudley Wood opened on 20 March to visitors Wolverhampton for a challenge match. Wolves' replacement for Ole was Jim McMillan who was a bonnie battler of vast experience, although it should be said that neither he nor fellow Scot George Hunter was able to kindle the emotions in the Cradley supporters as Warren and Olsen had before them.

Anyway, the first encounter led to a 45-33 victory for the Heathens, with all the team scoring well apart from young Wasley, who was left wondering where they had all gone to when the tapes went up. Nigel failed to score.

Two days later, United went to take their first look at the Brummies' track in another challenge match. Birmingham had joined the British League as National League Champions and, to their credit, had added only one established star to their ranks – the roly-poly Swede Soren Sjosten. They reckoned that they had stars of their own who could 'fly the flag', notably the Cradley management's friend, Arthur Browning, and the man that everybody was talking about – Birmingham youngster Alan Grahame. After a splendid match, the Brummies won by just 2 points, but Boulger showed his immediate liking for the track and registered his first maximum of the season.

In the return match at Dudley Wood the following weekend, Cradley won by 12 points, but although Boulger and Persson both scored double figures, Alan Grahame beat them both. The same could not be said of Dave Perks, however, who top-scored for United with a 12-point maximum. The Heathens got off to a cracking start in their League campaign at the end of the month by beating Leicester at Blackbird Road for the first time ever in the British League. Predictably, Boulger and Persson led the assault, scoring double figures, but the real match-winner was Nigel Wasley. He had failed to score a single point in the first three matches, and then scored a magnificent 9 points in this match to give United an 8-point victory.

The Heathens began April by losing to Coventry at Dudley Wood in the first leg of the Midland Cup, Boulger and Persson being the only Cradley riders to emerge with any credit. Bernie did beat Ole Olsen, but the team went into the return leg 8 points down. United lost by only 4 points at Poole, who were boasting one of the top riders in the League at that time in Malcolm Simmons. It was a match that saw Bruce Cribb in all kinds of trouble. He was still suffering from concussion that he had sustained against Birmingham, and the new regulation silencers were badly affecting his new four-valve machine. His low returns were reflecting his problems.

After beating Hackney at Dudley Wood, the Heathens were desperately unlucky not to take the points at Sheffield when Persson was excluded, Bastable fell and Boulger packed up when in front. As his bike ground to a halt, John received a nasty knock to his left knee, causing him to miss the next two matches. He managed to score only 6 points on the night, but Cribb came to the rescue, scoring 9 points and beginning his best patch of form ever for United.

In their next match, Cradley played host to Swindon and (without Boulger) scraped home by just 2 points, thanks to 17 points from Cribby. He top-scored again two nights later at Coventry in the return leg of the Midland Cup, and actually had six starts in the last seven heats! His efforts were in vain, however, and he lacked support as the Bees romped home 50-28.

The Heathens began May with a visit to high-flying Exeter and almost pulled off the shock result of the season. They were without Persson, but Boulger was back in the side. United went into heat five ahead by 6 points, but as Boulger chased Mauger home, a stone pierced his goggles and he was forced to withdraw from the meeting and was taken to hospital. Even so, Cradley held on and entered the final race on equal terms. The

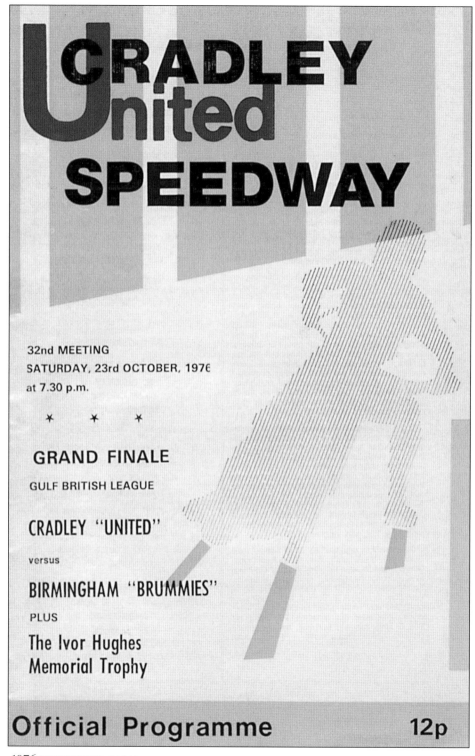

1976 programme cover.

Heathens' lowest scorers, Perks and Wasley, were unable to hold Scott Autrey and John Titman, and a brave battle was lost. Mauger had put in another unbeaten performance, but the stars of the night were Cribb, who scored 14 points, and Price, who burst into life, scoring 13 points.

Persson returned for the weekend when United faced Wolverhampton at Dudley Wood, but he had a poor match and the Heathens' supporters cringed as the old enemy nicked the match by 4 points, Cribb being the only Cradley rider to register double figures. The following Friday, United visited Monmore, and with Boulger returning, they lost by only 2 points. John made his comeback in the best possible way by scoring an immaculate maximum.

Wins at Dudley Wood, against White City and Newport, were followed by a defeat at Halifax that saw out the month for the Heathens. The last two matches had seen Cradley again without Persson, who had fled off to honour yet more of his foreign commitments. What had been a wonderful month for Bruce Cribb was eclipsed when he was runner-up to the unbeaten Malcolm Simmons in the LP Transport Trophy at Dudley Wood.

Boulger and Persson, although not setting the world alight, were riding well, but apart from these two and Cribb, the rest of the team were perilously inconsistent. Perks, Price and Bastable had all been up there with good scores, but they all seemed incapable of stringing together two or three good performances. It had not been a good month for Cradley, but it had been an even worse one for speedway. Wimbledon's dashing Swede Tommy Jansson had been killed racing in his homeland and was mourned by all in the sport.

The Heathens played 'Spot the Swede' in June. Out of the five matches in which they rode, Persson featured in only one – the last one in the month. United began the month playing host to Coventry, and as well as having Persson absent, they had to cope with Boulger being away riding in the World Pairs qualifier, as was Olsen for the Bees. The depleted teams rode to a draw in a match that saw the fiery Mitch Shirra lay his bike across the track after being excluded. Heated exchanges followed and the Coventry rider physically threatened poor old Vic White. Five days later, with Boulger back, Cradley lost by a single point at Ipswich in the first round of the Knockout Cup, guest Jimmy McMillan enjoying a fine match. United obviously fancied their chances in the return leg but, using rider replacement, they lost at home by 10 points and were out of the competition.

After losing at Hackney, the Heathens ended the month up at Kings Lynn. Persson, who was making his comeback, turned up late, and Boulger turned up even later! Both retired from the meeting, Boulger with machine troubles and Persson with sunstroke! It was no surprise that Cradley lost by 16 points, and they hovered uncertainly just below halfway in the League table.

July began with a surprising announcement by the Swedish speedway authorities that they had banned four-valve machines on their home tracks. After only four meetings, five riders had been taken to hospital and, what with the Jansson tragedy, they had decided that the machines had no place in their League. United's first match of the month was not until 10 July at Belle Vue, and in the interim, the rumours were flying thick and fast about the AWOL Persson. Cradley decided to rest Nigel Wasley and brought in New Zealander Paul Church for a few matches. He was at Belle Vue, but Bernie wasn't. Cradley got hammered.

A couple of nights later at Dudley Wood, it was announced that Bernt Persson would no longer be riding for Cradley. Following the death of his father-in-law, he would have to spend *more* time in Sweden to look after the family business – and anyway, he was now finding the financial rewards of riding in the British League unattractive. United were once again at the mercy of guest riders and rider replacement for the rest of the season. The boys responded by thrashing Poole. Arthur Price brought the house down when he beat Malcolm Simmons on the way to a glorious maximum, and Bastable chipped in with a useful 8 points. With Boulger scoring a steady 10 points, maybe all was not lost.

Price top-scored again in United's next match at home, when they beat Hull by a mere point. Arthur added Barry Briggs' scalp to his belt – twice. After beating Leicester, led by a Boulger maximum, Cradley had a couple of nasty shocks in the following two matches. Boulger crashed at Ipswich and was taken to hospital with internal bleeding, and two nights later at Dudley Wood, Bastable was leading Scott Autrey when the Heathens' frame snapped completely in half, throwing him heavily. Fortunately, neither rider was hurt badly and they missed no matches through their misadventures. United lost the Ipswich match, but despite Steve's bike disintegrating, United beat Exeter by 2 points, Mauger scoring the almost inevitable 15-point maximum.

Johnny Boulger made a very unfortunate exit at the Intercontinental final of the World Championship. After beating both Olsen and Mauger, his clutch burnt out at the gate in his last race, sending him through the tapes and out of the competition. He did, however, finish in fourth place in the Midland Riders' competition, but it was small consolation

1976 team line-up. From left to right: Arthur Price, Nigel Wasley (kneeling), Steve Bastable, John Boulger (on machine), Bruce Cribb, Dave Perks, Bernt Persson (kneeling), Vic White (manager). (www.mike-patrick.com)

Arthur Price. (Speedway Star)   *Bruce Cribb.* (Speedway Star)

indeed for the popular Australian. Persson also fell by the wayside and failed to reach the World final in what had been a very unsettling year for him to say the least.

United used a variety of guests throughout August and won all of their home matches, and even picked up a win away at Hull. Boulger had responded to Persson's absence and was back to his best, and young Nigel Wasley was back in the team and putting in some stirring performances. Price and Bastable were suffering from acute inconsistency and Perks was having a lean time, but Cradley were holding their own and maintained their mid-League position.

September was a milestone in British Speedway history. England had its first World Champion since Peter Craven back in 1962. Peter Collins of Belle Vue won the crown in Katowice, Poland with a thrilling display of riding. Not only that, but Malcolm Simmons took the runner-up spot, making it a double celebration for the Brits. Mauger had to settle for fourth place behind Phil Crump. Ironically, Collins' title was a testimony to Ivan Mauger. Peter was one of the youngsters that Ivan had taken under his wing in his days at Belle Vue when the Belle Vue Colts had started. Ivan the master had been beaten by the pupil.

Cradley had only three matches in September, all at Dudley Wood and all of which they won. They made a great start to October by beating visitors Kings Lynn, and Boulger lowered the track record to 66.0 seconds in the first race. By now, Cribb was back to his best, and in a match at Birmingham, which the Heathens won by 12 points, the referee excluded Bruce for tape-breaking in heat twelve. The Kiwi got the biggest cheer of the night when he stalked over to the starting lights and removed the offending exclusion bulb!

A narrow defeat at Swindon was followed by a visit to Monmore Green for the first leg of the Dudley/Wolves Trophy. Cradley elected to use rider replacement, and with Bastable giving one of his best displays of the season and Perks scoring well from the reserve

Steve Bastable. (Speedway Star)

berth, United came away from Wolverhampton with a 13-point lead. The return leg at Dudley Wood had to be cancelled in order for the Heathens to complete their league programme, and so United claimed the trophy. They finished off the league matches with wins against eventual Champions Ipswich, and Birmingham.

Despite all the upsets, Vic White had held the team together and they finished in a very creditable ninth place. John Boulger had played the captain's role and when it was needed, he upped his game to lead by example. He also pulled his average back up to almost 10 points. It had been Cribb's best year to date, and his 7.72 average was only so low due to his slow start to the season. Price had really shown what he could do in 1976, but he hadn't shown it often enough, and the result was a 5.7-point average.

Perks and Bastable both averaged 5.2 points, but they were the young blood of the team and would only improve. Bernie Persson had completed only nine League matches for Cradley in 1976 and had completely exasperated management and supporters alike, and his future at Dudley Wood looked grim.

Whatever the supporters thought was going to happen in 1977 was probably wrong. Nobody could have expected what was about to begin at Cradley. The Heathens were about to be taken on a ride. A ride that over the next few years would see them become possibly the best club side that speedway had ever seen.

THE HEATHENS THROUGH THE YEARS

(Averages shown in brackets)

1947   National League Division Three – Runners-up   (8 teams)

TEAM: Geoff Bennett (8.73), Les Beaumont (capt.) (8.15), Eric Irons (7.00), Jimmy Wright (6.50), Bob Fletcher (5.40), Ray Beaumont (4.45), Alan Hunt (3.88), Frank Evans (3.46), Phil Malpass (2.56), Wilf Wilstead (0.50).

MANAGER: George Buck

1948   National League Division Three – Runners-up   (13 teams)

TEAM: Gil Craven (8.75), Les Beaumont (capt.) (8.72), Eric Irons (8.23), Jimmy Wright (7.46), Alan Hunt (7.21), Bill Kemp (5.26), Ken Sharples (4.85), Jimmy Coy (4.50), Phil Malpass (4.20), Bill Clifton (4.20), Ray Beaumont (2.35), Roy Moreton (1.80), Frank Evans (1.66), Wilf Wilstead (1.40), Ted Moore (1.00).

MANAGER: George Buck

1949   National League Division Two – 4th place   (12 teams)

TEAM: Alan Hunt (9.16), Eric Williams (7.50), Gil Craven (6.51), Jack Arnfield (6.13), Roy Moreton (5.82), Geoff Godwin (4.47), Les Beaumont (4.16), Phil Malpass (4.06), Les Tolley (3.46), Bill Clifton (2.91), Bill Kemp (2.60), Ray Beaumont (2.00), Jim Pain (1.67).

MANAGER: Dudley Marchant

1950   National League Division Two – 3rd place   (15 teams)
         Midland Cup Winners

TEAM: Alan Hunt (10.04), Eric Boothroyd (6.65), Brian Shepherd (6.32), Phil Malpass (6.03), Gil Craven (5.92), Les Tolley (5.85), Laurie Schofield (3.83), Frank Young (3.40), Bill Clifton (3.35), Jack Arnfield (2.80), Harry Bastable (2.16), Jimmy Wright (1.00), Jim Pain (0.00).

MANAGER: Dicky Wise

1951   **National League Division Two – 15th place**   **(16 teams)**
            Central Shield Winners

TEAM: Gil Craven (capt.) (8.00), Phil Malpass (7.00), Guy Allott (6.16), Les Tolley (5.67), Harry Bastable (4.83), Laurie Schofield (4.20), Dick Tolley (4.20), Dennis Hitchings (2.32), Wilf Wilstead (2.27), Bill Clifton (2.18), Don Pettijohn (1.00).

MANAGER: Dicky Wise

1952   **National League Division Two – 4th place**   **(12 teams)**

TEAM: Harry Bastable (8.09), Brian Shepherd (7.52), Jim Tolley (6.23), Les Tolley (6.16), Phil Malpass (5.93), Fred Perkins (3.98), Geoff Bennett (3.69), Guy Allott (3.03), Laurie Schofield (2.50), Dick Tolley (2.45), Derek Braithwaite (2.25), Wilf Wilstead (1.00), Don Pettijohn (0.83).

MANAGER: Bill Sumner

1953 – 1959   **INACTIVE**

1960   **Provincial League – 6th place**   **(10 teams)**

TEAM: Harry Bastable (11.66), Eric Eadon (7.11), Ronnie Rolfe (capt.) (5.55), Roy Spencer (4.93), George Bewley (4.21), Vic White (4.07), Tony Eadon (1.93), Bill Coleman (3.60), Errol Brook (0.67).

MANAGER: Phil Malpass

1961   **Provincial League – 4th place**   **(11 teams)**
            Provincial League Cup Winners

TEAM: Ivor Brown (11.24), Harry Bastable (capt.) (10.09), Derek Timms (6.38), John Hart (4.54), Tony Eadon (4.28), Ivor Davies (6.57), Stan Stevens (8.50), Vic White (3.34), George Bewley (5.54), Ronnie Rolfe (5.13), Alan Totney (2.50), Eric Eadon (1.50), Mike Wilmore (1.00), Roy Spencer (0.50), Bruce Cooley (0.00).

MANAGER: Phil Malpass

1962   Provincial League – 8th place   **(13 teams)**

TEAM: Ivor Brown (10.8), Harry Bastable (capt.) (7.50), John Hart (6.00), Ivor Davies (5.00), Derek Timms (4.90), Nick Nichols (4.90), Stan Stevens (4.30), Alan Totney (2.30), George Bewley (1.80), John Belcher (1.50), Joe Westwood (1.00).

MANAGER: Roy Moreton

1963   Provincial League – 9th place   **(13 teams)**
              Provincial League Knockout Cup Winners
              Midland League Winners
              Dudley/Wolves Trophy Winners

TEAM: Ivor Brown (11.61), John Hart (8.42), Harry Bastable (capt.) (6.52), John Edwards (6.91), Alan Totney (6.32), Ivor Davies (4.76), Derek Timms (4.45), John Belcher (3.30), George Bewley (1.00), Joe Westwood (0.46), Eric Eadon (5.00), Dave Hankins (0.25).

MANAGER: Roy Moreton

1964   Provincial League – 10th place   **(12 teams)**

TEAM: Ivor Brown (capt.) (10.65), George Major (9.38), John Hart (8.25), Eric Hockaday (6.05), Harry Bastable (4.89), John Edwards (4.09), Alan Totney (4.02), Glyn Chandler (2.24), Matt Mattocks (2.00), Frank Holmes (1.46), Fred Priest (1.33), Derek Timms (1.25), John McGill (1.00), Errol Brook (1.00), Ivor Hughes (0.33), Ron Cooper (0.00).

MANAGER: Roy Moreton

1965   British League – 16th place   **(18 teams)**

TEAM: Ivor Brown (capt.) (10.00), John Hart (8.35), George Major (7.45), Leo McAuliffe (5.79), Eric Hockaday (5.55), Chris Julian (5.09), Harry Bastable (4.56), John Debbage (2.64), Ivor Hughes (2.17), Ron Cooper (0.86), Goog Allen (4.11), Tim Bungay (3.25), John Edwards (2.00), Matt Mattocks (1.20), Alan Totney (4.00).

MANAGER: Roy Moreton

1966   **British League – 19th place**   **(19 teams)**

TEAM: Ivor Brown (capt.) (7.88), Chris Julian (6.51), Chum Taylor (6.32), Clive Featherby (6.10), Ivor Hughes (5.65), Howard Cole (5.48), Eric Hockaday (3.64), Ron Cooper (3.58), Joe Weichbauer (2.40), Matt Mattocks (2.33), Ken Wakefield (2.00).

MANAGER: Roy Moreton, followed by Ted Flanaghan

1967   **British League – 18th place**   **(19 teams)**

TEAM: Ivor Brown (capt.) (7.47), Brian Brett (7.40), Tommy Bergqvist (7.28), Chris Julian (7.08), Jack Scott (6.37), Grahame Coombes (5.91), Jack Biggs (5.67), Alan Totney (3.76), Ken Wakefield (3.48), Peter Wrathall (3.16), Dave Schofield (2.89), Eric Hockaday (1.71).

MANAGER: Ted Flanaghan

1968   **British League – 14th place**   **(19 teams)**
             Dudley/Wolves Trophy Winners

TEAM: Roy Trigg (8.91), Bob Andrews (7.70), Grahame Coombes (6.71), Chris Julian (6.32), Lars Jansson (6.20), Ivor Brown (capt.) (5.68), Ken Wakefield (5.02). Tommy Bergqvist (5.02), Peter Wrathall (3.62), Archie Wilkinson (4.19), Alan Totney (3.16), Chris Hawkins (1.00).

MANAGER: Ted Flanaghan

1969   **British League – 7th place**   **(19 teams)**
             Dudley/Wolves Trophy Winners

TEAM: Roy Trigg (capt.) (9.27), Bernt Persson (9.11), Bob Andrews (7.93), Chris Bass (5.29), Grahame Coombes (4.90), Mike Gardner (4.31), Ken Wakefield (4.15), Peter Wrathall (2.50), Mike Holmes (2.00), Geoff Penniket (1.71), Chris Hawkins (1.29).

MANAGER: Ted Flanaghan

1970   British League – 15th place   **(19 teams)**

TEAM: Bernt Persson (9.29), Roy Trigg (8.45), Colin Pratt (capt.) (7.75), Jan Simensson (7.51), Chris Bass (4.38), Jimmy Squibb (4.09), Mike Gardner (3.50), Ken Wakefield (2.65), Glyn Chandler (2.00), Mike Holmes (1.60).

MANAGER: Russ Bragg

1971   British League – 18th place   **(19 teams)**
            Dudley/Wolves Trophy Winners

TEAM: Bernt Persson (9.68), Bob Andrews (7.73), Roy Trigg (capt.) (7.25), Pete Jarman (5.57), Jimmy Squibb (4.66), John Hart (4.25), Barry Duke (3.60), Bengt Andersson (2.11), Mick Handley (6.00), Richard Eslick (1.54), Cyril Francis (1.20), Andy Bearne (0.73).

MANAGER: Russ Bragg

1972   British League –16th place   **(18 teams)**

            Bernt Persson – World Championship Runner–up

TEAM: Bernt Persson (10.27), Bob Andrews (7.30), Roy Trigg (capt.) (6.96), Pete Jarman (4.90), John Hart (4.61), Mick Handley (4.57), Jimmy Squibb (3.73), Dave Perks (0.91), Ian Ross (2.00), Bengt Andersson (3.00), Dave Harvey (0.00) Gerald Smitherman (0.00).

MANAGER: Russ Bragg

1973   British League – 18th place   **(18 teams)**

TEAM: Bernt Persson (9.38), Howard Cole (9.12), Bruce Cribb (5.77), Colin Goody (4.84), Pete Jarman (4.49), Dave Perks (4.46), Malolm Corradine (4.40), Lars Hultberg (3.44), Ulf Lovaas (6.63), Brian Clarke (5.11), Dave Harvey (2.50).

MANAGER: Harry Bastable

1974   **British League – 13th place**   **(17 teams)**
               Dudley/Wolves Trophy Winners

TEAM: John Boulger (10.06), Howard Cole (capt.) (7.70), Bruce Cribb (6.19), Sandor Levai (5.79), Arthur Price (5.56), Russell Osborne (4.70), Malcolm Corradine (4.14), Dave Perks (4.00), Steve Bastable (2.09), Dave Younghusband (3.33), Alan Molyneux (5.71) , Phil Bass (2.29).

MANAGER: Harry Bastable

1975   **British League – 11th place**   **(18 teams)**

TEAM: John Boulger (capt.) (8.73), Bernt Persson (8.58), Arthur Price (7.68), Bruce Cribb (7.53), Sandor Levai (4.87), Steve Bastable (4.84), Dave Perks (4.56), Russell Osborne (3.08), Kevin Mullarkey (3.08), Dave Younghusband (3.33), Alan Molyneux (5.71) , Phil Bass (2.29).

MANAGER: Peter Worthington

1976   **British League – 9th place**   **(19 teams)**
               Dudley/Wolves Trophy Winners

               John Boulger – Australasian Champion

TEAM: John Boulger (capt.) (9.76), Bernt Persson (9.16), (withdrew) Bruce Cribb (7.72), Arthur Price (5.71), Steve Bastable (5.20), Nigel Wasley (3.16), Paul Church (0.00).

MANAGER: Vic White